Allah's name I begin with,
the utmost Kind, the ever Merciful.

# I am a British Muslim

## MY RIGHTS AND RESPONSIBILITIES

Muhammad Imdad Hussain Pirzada

AL-KARAM
PUBLICATIONS

ISBN 978 0 9569388 5 5

First Edition 2014 (3000)

Published by
Al-Karam Publications Ltd
Eaton Hall, Retford, Nottinghamshire, DN22 0PR, England, United Kingdom
www.alkarampublications.com

Edited, designed and typeset by Bakhtyar H Pirzada al-Azhari
info@alkarampublications.com

Printed and bound in the United Kingdom by
Midland Regional Printers Ltd, Nottingham

Printed on recycled, FSC or virgin material from well managed forests

Cover photograph:
A photo of the Faizan-e-Madinah Masjid in Peterborough.


Abbreviations used in the book:
   🌸    *salla'Llahu 'alayhi wa sallam*, Allah bless him and grant him peace.
   [*as*]    *alayhi'l-salam*, upon him be peace.
   [*ra*]    *radiya'Llahu anhu/anha*, Allah be pleased with him/her.

To all citizens of the
United Kingdom of Great Britain and Northern Ireland.

*'Peace cannot be kept by force.*
*It can only be achieved by understanding.'*

The beloved Prophet Muhammad ﷺ said:

"None of you can become a (true) believer until he loves for all people
what he loves for himself."

[*Musnad Ahmad ibn Hanbal*, vol. 3, p. 272]

In light of this prophetic command, I sincerely pray, O my Lord!
In all Muslim and non-Muslim countries of the world including Britain,
remove *zulm* (tyranny) and terrorism, and bring justice and security,
remove hypocrisy and falsehood, and bring sincerity and truthfulness,
so that all people in this global village of ours
can live a peaceful life with freedom. *Amin.*

*Muhammad Imdad Hussain Pirzada*

# Contents

# Endorsements

MUHAMMAD IMDAD HUSSAIN Pirzada is a known writer having authored numerous books covering a vast array of topics. He is a leading and important scholarly voice for the community. 'I am a British Muslim' is a timely and much welcomed contribution of his, which is straightforward and concise. It is my pleasure to endorse this book which takes the reader down memory lane into the contributions of Muslims in Europe, from the influences of Muslim Spain to the very presence of Muslims here in Great Britain. It further concisely yet scholarly elaborates upon the Islamic teachings in relation to the state, the population and the sense of civic duty. With focus on the responsibilities of Muslims, it provides good counsel for the community in developing positive relations towards building a cohesive society and also highlights the rights of the community, especially in the face of Islamophobia as well as various other challenges of the present day.

Our lives and identities can no longer be defined through the ethnic origin or countries from where the first generations migrated from. We are firmly British and firmly Muslim. This is our identity. Great Britain is our country and members of various communities within Great Britain are our neighbours and together we are citizens of the same state. It is our obligation, as British Muslims, to fathom our rights as well as our responsibilities and to contribute fully and wholeheartedly towards this society. And for this, Muhammad Imdad Hussain Pirzada has presented a beneficial and much needed book which needs to be read and understood by all. I admire and applaud this work and I am grateful to him for putting his pen to paper on this topic and providing his insight.

Therefore, I am delighted to endorse 'I am a British Muslim'.

*Lord Nazir Ahmed of Rotherham*

'I AM A BRITISH Muslim' is a new book authored by the renowned academic, educationist and scholar; Allama Muhammad Imdad Hussain Pirzada. Though the author has dedicated this book to all the citizens of the United Kingdom, after reading this wonderful work, I believe that this book should be read by everybody in the West. The book begins with a chapter on Muslims in Spain in which the author has brilliantly outlined the unique feature of Spanish society under Muslim rule, where Jews, Christians and Muslims lived together peacefully. This motivates and inspires the cohesion, coexistence and mutual respect needed in the United Kingdom today. The author has also discussed constructively the role Muslims should play in shaping the future of Britain. Such a reality would help to create a Muslim community that can participate in and contribute richly to British society and culture. Similarly the issues of rights, responsibilities, tolerance and duty towards neighbours have been presented eloquently which certainly makes this work positive and interestingly unique. The book also debates honestly and openly the role of Imams and community leaders, which is in my opinion essential for the effective growth and development of the Muslim community.

Under the present climate of Islamophobia, misunderstanding and confusion about Islam and Muslims, I would strongly recommend that this book is widely circulated and read throughout the Western world by all those who are engaged in a variety of community activities. Particularly I hope that young Muslims may certainly benefit from this tremendous work.

*Maulana Mohammad Shahid Raza OBE*
*Head Imam, Leicester Central Mosque, Leicester*
*President, World Islamic Mission, European Region*

IN THIS TIMELY new book, Muhammad Imdad Hussain Pirzada presents Islam's vision for a coherent society, using a wide range of classical Muslim resources.

*Shaykh Abdal Hakim Murad (T. J. Winter)*
*Shaykh Zayed Lecturer of Islamic Studies, University of Cambridge*
*Dean, The Cambridge Muslim College*

THIS IS AN uncomplicated and nourishing book whose contents have been selected from a storehouse of knowledge which provides much food for thought and reflection. It reminds me of the saying attributed to Pythagoras, "Life is a journey, so make the most of whatever company in which you find yourself." In seeking to remind every citizen, not only of Great Britain but indeed of the world, of our basic rights and responsibilities, especially towards our creator and towards each other, Shaykh Muhammad Imdad Hussain Pirzada also graphically reminds us that in every age

Allah has spread the life-transaction of Islam by means of those who reject Islam as well as through those who accept Islam – and that in every age Islam has been established by the sword of wisdom, which effortlessly removes the veils of ignorance and arrogance which always seek to hide and misrepresent the truth. As William Blake observed, "Without contraries is no progression." I guarantee that you will learn something from this book which you did not know before!

*Hajj Ahmad Thomson*
*Author and Barrister*

# Preface

GREAT BRITAIN IS a multi-cultural, multi-racial and multi-religious country with a diverse population. One segment of the British society is the community of Muslims who are the largest faith community in the country after the Christians.

In maintaining a harmonious and peaceful society in which each individual is respected, there lies great responsibility on all factions of the society, from the government to the populace and from the communities to the individuals. In this respect, I decided to write a concise and straightforward book for British Muslims in particular, and the British community in general, with the aim of increasing knowledge and understanding by realising basic rights and responsibilities.

In this book, I have indicated towards certain elements within Great Britain that are somewhat similar to Islamic teachings. This does not mean, however, that there is all Islam in this country. In reality, there are many things that do not conform to Islamic teachings, however British Muslims enjoy greater rights and freedoms here than in any other country. It is true that time and again, voices are raised against the Muslim community from various corners highlighting weaknesses and flaws within the community. Therefore, it is essential that British Muslims eradicate the wrongs within them and convince those in authority that British Muslims are lawful citizens of this country and, hence, their rights should be protected and further rights given. If the community does not eradicate the blemishes that tarnish its standing within the society, this will have negative effects on the coming generation and possibly citizenship of this country may end for some. Nonetheless, if British Muslims remove the black sheep from within them through mutual unity and whilst remaining firm on their religion strengthen their economic, social and political state, then their future will only get better and prosperous.

I have begun this book with a brief glance into history and specifically the glorious era of Muslim rule in Spain which continued for eight centuries. The story of Muslims in Europe is not a new story and Muslim Spain is a chapter that cannot be ignored for this was a time and place of great human values, dignity and tolerance of difference and it was also the moment of great intellectual and scientific endeavour which paved the way forward and contributed to the world we enjoy today. The end of this period in history with the expulsion of the Muslims from Spain is also a moment worthy of reflection, for history teaches lessons.

Moving on from the story of Muslim Spain, I have looked at the significant moments of Islam's presence and the interaction of the Muslims in Great Britain. No doubt that the greater influx of Muslim immigrants occurred during the second half of the last century, nonetheless there have been important contributions in relation to Islam and the country of Great Britain that occurred much prior to this time. It is worth having a little knowledge of these times, places and people and their contributions.

As this book is primarily intended for British Muslims, the focus of the subsequent chapters remains on understanding duties and responsibilities in light of the teachings of Islam. Muslims are to take guidance from their religion as Islam is a complete code of life that has lessons in it for every individual and community and for each situation and circumstance. If British Muslims fully implement the values and teachings of the Qur'an and the beloved Prophet Muhammad ﷺ in their characters, conducts and lives, they will most certainly find light in difficult times.

Towards the end of this book, I have made mention of some of the difficulties faced by British Muslims and it is their right and the duty of the governing authorities, in particular the British Government, to address these imbalances so that the country prospers further and remains harmonious and at peace within. I have also included some points in relation to the popular objections raised against the Muslims and their faith so that the Muslims feel confident with their faith and those raising baseless objections can too genuinely reflect and put an end to negative propaganda against a people and their religion.

*Muhammad Imdad Hussain Pirzada*
*21 February 2014*
*Jamia Al-Karam, England*

# CHAPTER 1

# Muslim Spain

THE HISTORY OF Spain (*al-Andalus*, Andalusia) is quite peculiar and strange. Most of the time, outside nations and foreign rulers occupied this land, who often remained in a state of warfare and struggle with each other. The essayist of *The New Universal Encyclopedia* in his detailed analysis writes:

> The Visigothic kingdom of Spain, established about 530 by a new effort on the part of that race, lasted for nearly two hundred years. It was not a strong one, however, an elective monarchy being one cause of its weakness, and religious dissensions another. The quarrel between the Arians and believers in the orthodox faith was acute. King Recared, at a council of Toledo in 589, declared the Catholic faith to be the national religion, but the Arians were by no means crushed.[1]

## The arrival of Muslims in Spain

It was as a result of the internal rivalry and conflict taking place in Spain that one of the two rival kings invited the Muslims to Spain in order to help and assist him in his struggle. The essayist of *The*

*New Universal Encyclopedia* highlighting this writes:

> The fall of the Visigothic kingdom was due to its internal dissensions. Two rival kings were chosen and one of them looked to Africa for help. At his invitation a band of Muslims arrived in 711 and Roderic, the last Visigothic king, fell in battle. These Muslims were followed by others, and very soon Spain was in Muslim possession.[2]

This is that legendary episode when Tariq ibn Ziyad (d. 720), accompanied by seven thousand soldiers, passed through Morocco and crossed the narrow strait that connects the Atlantic Ocean to the Mediterranean Sea referred to as the 'Strait of Gibraltar'. The name 'Gibraltar' itself stems from the Arabic words *jabal tariq* referring to the 'mountain of Tariq'. It is well-known that when Tariq ibn Ziyad crossed the strait and landed on the shores of Spain, he set fire to all his boats and ships so that the soldiers could no longer contemplate retreat from battle and, with full zeal and passion for martyrdom, they struggle with all that they have. Soon, reinforcements of a further five thousand soldiers also arrived.

Consequently, the Islamic conquests of Spain began in 711 when Tariq ibn Ziyad with only twelve thousand Muslim soldiers defeated the Spanish army of one hundred thousand soldiers and headed towards Cordoba. Thereafter, Muslims ruled over Spain for nearly eight hundred years.

## The advancement of Muslim Spain

In Spain, the Muslims built impressive palaces, roads, boulevards, mosques, seminaries and medical centres. An effective mailing and postal system was introduced. A naval fleet was established to defend the country and factories for producing armoury and weaponry were constructed. Bridges were erected over rivers and a system of irrigation of water was put in place to promote agriculture. There was no electricity at that time, the Muslims of Spain achieved this through the flowing of water. They would construct different types of dams and barriers for the rivers and waterways, thereby raising the water level high above the surface and then cause it to fall. With the tremendous energy produced by this fall and flowing of water, they would power and run their factories and workshops. During that age, Spain advanced immensely in the manufacturing of clothing. The number of factories for producing silk alone was eight hundred. The most beautiful and delicate paper of the world was then produced in Spain. The machines used to produce such quality paper were also powered by the force of water. Attractive and fragile utensils and pottery made from glass, ceramic and metal were all made in Spain then exported and sold throughout the world.[3]

HRH the Prince of Wales, Charles, has acknowledged this reality when he so well said:

> Many of the traits on which modern Europe prides itself came to it from Muslim Spain. Diplomacy, free trade, open borders, the techniques of academic research, of anthropology, etiquette, fashion, various types of medicine, hospitals, all came from this great city of cities [Cordoba]... The surprise is the extent to which Islam has been a part of Europe for so long, first in Spain, then in the Balkans, and the extent to which it has contributed so much towards the civilization which we all too often think of, wrongly, as entirely Western. Islam is part of our past and our present, in all fields of human endeavour. It has helped to create modern Europe. It is part of our own inheritance, not a thing apart.[4]

## The educational revolution in Muslim Spain

No historian of the world, from whichever religious or geographical background, can deny the fact that when Muslims came to Spain, all of Europe was covered in the darkness of ignorance. There was no scholar nor doctor, and no alchemist nor scientist.

As soon as the Muslims arrived, they radically changed the state and condition and everywhere lit candles of knowledge and skills. The Muslim sovereigns of Spain were themselves great scholars and patrons of knowledge and education. Al-Muzaffar (d. 1008) authored an encyclopaedia consisting of fifty volumes and there were four hundred thousand books in the library of al-Hakam II (d. 976). There was no community nor settlement in Spain in which there was no library. In the twelfth century, there were one thousand such large seminaries and centres of learning in Cordoba where secondary and higher education was provided. With each university, large libraries were also established in which thousands of books could be found on each and every topic.[5]

HRH the Prince of Wales has elaborated on this point with the words:

> If there is much misunderstanding in the West about the nature of Islam, there is also much ignorance about the debt our own culture and civilization owe to the Islamic world. It is a failure which stems, I think, from the straightjacket of history which we have inherited. The medieval Islamic world, from Central Asia to the shores of the Atlantic, was a world where scholars and men of learning flourished. But because we have tended to see Islam as the enemy of the West, as an alien culture, society, and system of belief, we have

tended to ignore or erase its great relevance to our own history. For example, we have underestimated the importance of eight hundred years of Islamic society and culture in Spain between the eighth and fifteenth centuries. The contribution of Muslim Spain to the preservation of classical learning during the Dark Ages, and to the first flowerings of the Renaissance, has long been recognized. But Islamic Spain was much more than a mere larder where Hellenistic knowledge was kept for later consumption by the emerging modern Western world. Not only did Muslim Spain gather and preserve the intellectual content of ancient Greek and Roman civilization, it also interpreted and expanded upon that civilization, and made a vital contribution of its own in so many fields of human endeavour – in science, astronomy, mathematics, algebra (itself an Arabic word), law, history, medicine, pharmacology, optics, agriculture, architecture, theology, music. Averroes [Ibn Rushd] and Avenzoar [Ibn Zuhr], like their counterparts Avicenna [Ibn Sina] and Rhazes [Razi] in the East, contributed to the study and practice of medicine in ways from which Europe benefited for centuries afterwards.

Islam nurtured and preserved the quest for learning. In the words of the tradition, 'the ink of the scholar is more sacred than the blood of the martyr.' Cordoba in the tenth century was by far the most civilized city of Europe. We know of lending libraries in Spain at the time King Alfred was making terrible blunders with the culinary arts in this country. It is said that the 400,000 volumes in its ruler's library amounted to more books than all the libraries of the rest of Europe put together. That was made possible because the Muslim world acquired from China the skill of making paper more than four hundred years before the rest of non-Muslim Europe.[6]

The following are names of some of the scholars and polymaths who substantially contributed towards education, science, philosophy, research, etc., from Muslim Spain:

1.  Ibn Rushd (1126-1198). He was born in Cordoba and was an important jurist and *qadi* (judge) of Cordoba. He was a leading scientist and a scholar of Arabic Philosophy. He is also known by the name 'Averroes' in the West.

2.  Ibn Hazm (994-1064). He was born in Cordoba and authored around four hundred books covering various disciplines including history, philosophy, psychology, ethics, etc.

3.  Abu'l-Qasim al-Zahrawi (936-1013). He was a leading physician and surgeon of Muslim Spain with pioneering contributions to the field of surgical procedures and instruments. He is the founding father of modern surgery. He is also known by the name 'Albucasis' in the West.

4.  Ibn 'Abd al-Barr (978-1071). He was counted amongst the great jurists and Islamic scholars of Cordoba.

5.  Abu Hayyan al-Gharnati (1256-1344). He was born in Granada. He was a scholar recognised as an expert Arabic linguist who authored books covering the disciplines of etymology, syntax, jurisprudence and rhetoric. His greatest work is his linguistics commentary of the Qur'an, *al-Bahr al-Muhit*.

6.   Abu 'Abdullah al-Qurtubi (1214-1273). He was a well-known and famous Islamic scholar who authored many books. His greatest and famous work is his commentary of the Qur'an, *Tafsir al-Qurtubi*.

7.   Ibn Juljul (943-1010). He was an influential physician and pharmacologist of Cordoba. He wrote an extensive and significant work on the history of medicine, *Tabaqat al-Atibba' wa'l-Hukama'*.

8.   Ibn Tufayl (1100-1186). He was a famous philosopher, physician and novelist of Granada.

9.   Ibn al-Khatib (1314-1375). He was a resident of Granada. He authored around sixty books on various topics including literature, philosophy, spirituality, history, geography and medicine.

10.  Ibn al-Wafid (997-1074). He was the prominent researcher of pharmacology in Spain. He is also known by the name 'Abenguefit' in the West.

## The establishment of universities in England and Europe

In the flagship publication of the international science and cultural heritage brand, *1001 Inventions*, titled *Muslim Heritage in Our World*, it states:

> The oldest English and European universities, where some of us receive our undergraduate and postgraduate degrees, started to appear in the 12th century... The influx of these Muslim tomes of knowledge, which explored the world and heavens in a rational way, meant that new institutions appeared

in Europe... Many historians today say that the blueprints of the earliest English universities, like Oxford, came with these travelling, open-minded scholars and returning crusaders who, as well as visiting Muslim universities in places like Cordoba, brought back the translated books based on rational thought and not prophecy.[7]

## Muslim Spain was home to Jews, Christians and Muslims

*The New Encyclopaedia Britannica* categorically mentions that Medieval Spain, with its large Muslim and Jewish populations, 'was the only multi-racial and multi-religious country in western Europe, and much of the development of Spanish civilization in religion, literature, art, and architecture during the later Middle Ages stemmed from this fact'.[8]

The publication *Muslim Heritage in Our World* of the *1001 Inventions* states:

In 12th century Toledo at least three cultures lived side by side: Muslims, Jews and Christians. This was a time of cultural richness where all shared the same, breath-taking desire for knowledge... The real jewel of Toledo is to be found in the city's libraries and involved all three communities (Muslims, Jews and Christians) working in a particular field, translation... It was in 12th century Toledo that possibly the greatest translation effort, from Arabic to Latin, in the history of science took place, which attracted every single-minded scholar and translator of the Christian West.[9]

Just as Muslims, Jews and Christians lived with one another in Spain and all of them together contributed to the advancement of

Spain, similarly there is a need today for us – Muslims, Jews, Christians, Hindus, Sikhs, Buddhists, etc. – to collectively play our fulfilling role towards the advancement of Great Britain.

## The end of the Muslims and the Jews in Spain

When the Christians gained control over Granada after defeating the Muslim ruler in 1492, the Catholic Monarchs (King Ferdinand II and Queen Isabella I) subjected the Muslims to unyielding levels of tyranny and oppression. A campaign of forcefully converting the Muslims to Christianity was initiated. They were killed for trivial reasons and their properties were seized. Religious courts of Spain began ordering their execution by being burned alive. For nearly a century, the Christian rulers of Spain exposed the Muslims to their inhumane and callous tyranny and as such the Muslims, who had governed Spain with full pomp and glory for nearly eight hundred years, had suddenly been erased like a mistaken letter.

This is a harsh yet historical fact. In 1609, the Christian rulers ordered the Muslims to leave Spain all together at once. Since the Christian rulers had been inflicting atrocious cruelty and merciless oppression on the Muslims for a century, thousands of Muslims left and migrated towards Africa. From the seven hundred mosques that were built in Cordoba, today only one survives and even that has been turned into a museum.[10]

*The New Encyclopaedia Britannica* states, "During the reign of the Catholic Monarchs several thousand *conversos* were condemned and burned for Judaizing practices. Many more thousands of *conversos* escaped similar fates only by fleeing the country."[11]

## A contrast in religious tolerance

HRH the Prince of Wales, pointing towards the contrast between

Muslim Spain and that which followed afterwards, stated:

> Medieval Islam was a religion of remarkable tolerance
> for its time, allowing the Jews and Christians the right
> to practise their inherited beliefs, and setting an
> example which was not, unfortunately, copied for
> many centuries in the West.[12]

Ahmad Hemaya in his book *Islam: A Profound Insight*, a book
certified by Al-Azhar in Egypt, correctly wrote:

> The centuries-long existence of non-Muslims
> throughout the Muslim world, from Moorish Spain
> and Africa, south of the Sahara, to Egypt, Syria, India
> and Indonesia, is a clear proof of the religious
> tolerance of Islam towards people of different
> religions. This tolerance even led to the annihilation of
> Muslims, like in Spain, where the remaining
> Christians took advantage of the Muslim weakness.
> The Christians attacked them there and practiced
> forced conversions, expulsion and murder until the
> last Muslim was exterminated.[13]

The British Orientalist Sir Thomas Arnold wrote:

> We hear nothing of any organised attempt to force the
> acceptance of Islam on the non-Muslim population, or
> of any systematic persecution intended to stamp out
> the Christian religion. Had the Caliphs chosen to
> adopt either course of action, they might have swept
> away Christianity as easily as Ferdinand and Isabella
> drove Islam out of Spain, or as Louis XIV made
> Protestantism penal in France, or as the Jews were
> kept out of England for 350 years... The very survival

of these Churches to the present day is a strong proof of the generally tolerant attitude of the Mohammedan governments towards them.[14]

On the theme of religious tolerance during Muslim rule in history, Professor Nabil Matar in his book *Islam in Britain: 1558-1685* writes:

In Smyrna [present day Izmir in Turkey], in the second half of the seventeenth century, there were mosques, synagogues, Roman Catholic, Greek Orthodox and Armenian churches, along with Protestant chapels – demonstrating a religious tolerance that was unparalleled in the cities of western Christendom. Even today, after four hundred years of Ottoman rule of the Middle East, many parts of the former Empire (particularly in the Eastern Mediterranean) have maintained sizeable minorities of Christians.[15]

Whilst discussing the religious tolerance of Islam and the 'Golden Age', in particular the Muslim attitude towards the Jews over the course of history, the Israeli writer and journalist Uri Avnery rejects the notion of Islam spreading by the sword. He writes:

There is no evidence whatsoever of any attempt to impose Islam on the Jews. As is well known, under Muslim rule the Jews of Spain enjoyed a bloom the like of which the Jews did not enjoy anywhere else until almost our time. Poets like Yehuda Halevy wrote in Arabic, as did the great Maimonides. In Muslim Spain, Jews were ministers, poets, and scientists. In Muslim Toledo, Christian, Jewish and Muslim scholars worked together and translated the ancient Greek philosophical and scientific texts. That was, indeed, the Golden Age. How would this have been possible if the Prophet decreed the 'spreading of the faith by the sword'? What happened afterwards is even more telling. When the Catholics re-conquered Spain from the Muslims, they instituted a reign of religious terror. The Jews and the Muslims were presented with a cruel choice: to become Christians, to be massacred or to leave. And where did the hundreds of thousands of Jews, who refused to abandon their faith, escape? Almost all of them were received with open arms in the Muslim countries... Every honest Jew who knows the history of his people cannot but feel a deep sense of gratitude to Islam, which has protected the Jews for fifty generations, while the Christian world persecuted the Jews and tried many times 'by the sword' to get them to abandon their faith.[16]

Ahmad Hemaya further commented on the Muslim protection provided to the Jews during the middle of the twentieth century, he wrote:

On November 2, 2007, the Jewish-American photographer Norman Gershman held an exhibition in the Holocaust Memorial of Jerusalem in Yad Vashem. This exhibit documented how the Muslims of Albania in the period of 1943-45, in spite of all dangers, provided hundreds of Jews from many countries protection from the Nazis, gave them hideouts in their homes and thus saved them. From the published documents from Albania one can see that practically all Jews who sought refuge in the country were saved.[17]

## Notes

1   Alfonso Lopez, 'Spain; its history and its peoples', *The New Universal Encyclopedia*, ed. by Sir John Hammerton and Gordon Stowell (London: The Caxton Publishing Company Limited), vol. 14, p. 7690.

2   ibid.

3   Sayyid Qasim Mahmood, *Islami Encyclopaedia*, 8th edition (Lahore: Al-Faysal), vol. 1, pp. 283-284.

4   H.R.H. The Prince of Wales, *Islam and the West*, a lecture given in the Sheldonian Theatre, Oxford, on 27 October 1993 (Oxford: Oxford Centre for Islamic Studies, 1993), p. 18.

5   Sayyid Qasim Mahmood, *Islami Encyclopaedia*, vol. 1, p. 283.

6   H.R.H. The Prince of Wales, *Islam and the West*, pp. 17-18.

7   'European Universities', *1001 Inventions: Muslim Heritage in Our World*, 2nd edition, ed. by Salim T S Al-Hassani, (Manchester: Foundation for Science, Technology and Civilisation Ltd, 2007), pp. 96-98.

8   *The New Encyclopaedia Britannica*, 15th edition (Chicago: Encyclopaedia Britannica, Inc., 1995), vol. 28, p. 38.

9   'Translating Knowledge', *1001 Inventions: Muslim Heritage in Our World*, pp. 93, 94.

10   Sayyid Qasim Mahmood, *Islami Encyclopaedia*, vol. 1, p. 284.

11   *The New Encyclopaedia Britannica*, vol. 28, p. 39.

12   H.R.H. The Prince of Wales, *Islam and the West*, p. 18.

13   Ahmad M. Hemaya, *Islam: A Profound Insight* (Cairo: Zamzam Presses, 2011), p. 324.

14   Cited in Ahmad M Hemaya, *Islam: A Profound Insight*, p. 325.

15   Nabil Matar, *Islam in Britain: 1558-1685* (New York: Cambridge University Press, 1998), p. 29.

16   Cited in Ahmad M Hemaya, *Islam: A Profound Insight*, pp. 333-334.

17   Ahmad M Hemaya, *Islam: A Profound Insight*, p. 335.

# CHAPTER 2

# Islam in Great Britain

BY VIRTUE OF the 1536 Act of Union, England and Wales came together in a political and legal union and then with the Acts of Union of 1707, England and Scotland merged together into a single kingdom named 'Great Britain'. Later, through the Act of Union of 1801, Great Britain united with Ireland under the name of the 'United Kingdom'. This union remained until the Anglo-Irish Treaty of 1921, which came to effect following the Irish War of Independence and resulted in the formation of the Republic of Ireland. However, Northern Ireland remained, thereby resulting in the 'United Kingdom of Great Britain and Northern Ireland'.

Today, the United Kingdom consists of England, Wales, Scotland and Northern Ireland, and Britain consists of England, Wales and Scotland. The terms 'Britain' and 'Great Britain' are often used synonymously with 'United Kingdom'.[1]

## Islam and Britain

The connection between Great Britain and Islam is quite old and longstanding. It began during the time when the English began travelling to Africa and the Middle East for the purposes of business and trade.

Some passages from *Islam in Britain: 1558-1685* by Professor Nabil Matar are presented here to shed light on this history:

> Indeed, of all the countries of Europe, Britain enjoyed the most extensive trade with the Muslim Empire in the seventeenth century... By the end of the seventeenth century, trade with Turkey accounted, according to Sir John Chardin, for one quarter of all England's overseas commercial activity... Although geographically far from the Ottoman Empire, England and the rest of the British Isles produced numerous converts who later settled in that Empire... Islamic society, as numerous visitors noted, was powerful and well-knit because it combined religious law with civil life. To live in the Ottoman Empire, particularly in the large urban centres, invariably led to engagement with the traditions, celebrations and feasts of Islam... Islam overpowered Englishmen by the force of cultural habit.[2]

> The first English convert to Islam whose name survives in an English source, *The voyage made to Tripolis* (1583), was a servant, 'a son of a yeoman of our Queen's Guard... His name was John Nelson.'[3]

> In his autobiography, Pitts[4] mentioned an 'Irish Renegado' who had made the pilgrimage to Mecca and an Englishman by the name of James Grey who converted to Islam and became so well-versed in Islamic lore that he became 'a Zealot.'[5]

From 1707 onwards, Great Britain began to take shape and come into existence. It is understood from this that even before the establishment of Great Britain, Islam was already present here.

Furthermore, Islam is equally part of the present development of Great Britain and has contributed to its advancement as well.

## The education and propagation of Islam in Britain

From 1960 onwards, the majority of Muslims came to Great Britain in pursuit of education and a better livelihood, and then they settled here. Wherever a believer goes, his or her faith firmly remains accompanying. Consequently, alongside livelihood and education, the Muslims here accomplished prominent endeavours and praiseworthy deeds in the education and propagation of Islam. With their hard-earned income, they built mosques, seminaries, centres of learning and schools in which our coming generations are acquiring an Islamic education. The religious leadership i.e. scholars, elders and teachers as well as the common folk i.e. labourers, professionals and businessmen, have all played a tremendous role in this endeavour.

## The establishing of mosques in Britain

The first mosque in Great Britain is recorded as having been established in 1860 at 2 Glynrhondda Street in Cathays, Cardiff. Then the first purpose-built mosque of Great Britain, The Shah Jahan Mosque, was constructed in 1889 in Woking, Surrey. Today there are over fifteen hundred mosques in Great Britain and with the growth in the Muslim population every year, the number of mosques is also on the increase.

## The locals accepting Islam

Islam is a natural religion and has ample potential to fulfil the requirements of every age. For this reason, even in developed countries such as in America and Europe, the religion growing the fastest at present is Islam. Thousands of locals and natives of Great Britain have also accepted Islam. Over the past century or so, the names Quilliam and Pickthall stand out amongst the influential converts who contributed to Islam and the Muslims:

1.  *Shaykh Abdullah Quilliam*
    Most prominent and historically significant among the local converts to Islam is William Henry Quilliam (1856-1932), who began work as a solicitor in Liverpool and who accepted Islam in 1887 at the age of 31, taking the name Abdullah Quilliam.[6] His conversion led to a remarkable story of the growth of Islam in Victorian Britain. Quilliam was appointed *Shaykh al-Islam* of the British Isles in 1894 by the last Ottoman Caliph, Sultan Abdul Hamid II. He established the Liverpool Muslim Institute and Mosque at 8 Brougham Terrace, West Derby Road, Liverpool, and later purchased the remainder of the terrace, establishing a boarding school for boys and a day school for girls. He also opened an orphanage (Medina House) for non-Muslim children whose parents could not look after them, and agreed for them to be raised in the values of Islam. Quilliam's propagation of Islam led to around six hundred people in the United Kingdom embracing Islam, many of them very educated and prominent individuals in British society, as well as ordinary men and women. He passed away in 1932 and was buried in the Muslim cemetery at Brookwood near Woking, Surrey, where Abdullah Yusuf Ali, Muhammad Marmaduke Pickthall and Lord Headley are also buried.[7]

2.  *Muhammad Pickthall*
    Another significant convert who accepted Islam in 1917 is Muhammad Marmaduke Pickthall (1875-1936). He is one of the earliest translators of the Qur'an in English. His work is

titled *The Meaning of the Glorious Qur'an* and it was the first translation done by a Muslim whose native language was English. He passed away in 1936.

The names of some of the notable contemporary individuals who have embraced Islam include Abdal Hakim Murad (Timothy J. Winter), Yusuf Islam (Cat Stevens), Dr Abdalqadir as-Sufi (Ian Dallas), Ahmad Thomson, Abdalhaqq Bewley, Aisha Bewley, Lauren Booth (sister-in-law of former British Prime Minister Tony Blair) and Yvonne Ridley among others.

## Allama Iqbal and Britain

Not only have individuals from Great Britain accepted Islam over the years and contributed to the religion of Islam and the affairs of the Muslims, there have also been important and influential Muslim figures and personalities from outside Great Britain who have had a connection with this country. Highly significant amongst them is Allama Muhammad Iqbal (1877-1938), the renowned poet-philosopher of Islam about who Justice Shaykh Muhammad Karam Shah in his essay *Iqbal's Concept of Love* wrote, "The existence of Iqbal is such an immense blessing from Allah that the Muslim nation can never discharge itself from the duty of demonstrating gratitude for it."[8]

Allama Iqbal is an influential Muslim of the last century whose contributions towards the religion of Islam and the then prevailing condition of Muslims around the world, in particular those of the Indian Subcontinent, are many and worthy of contemplation. In 1905, Iqbal came to Great Britain for higher study and research at Cambridge. In his three years of stay in Europe, Iqbal obtained a BA from the University of Cambridge (1906), qualified as a barrister at London's Middle Temple (1906) and earned a PhD from Ludwig Maximilian University of Munich, in Germany

(1908).[9] Iqbal's poetry in Urdu and Persian gained prominence during his lifetime and found lecturers at the University of Cambridge translating his poetic books into English, such as Reynold A. Nicholson and Arthur J. Arberry. When the poetry and works of Iqbal continued to gain popularity worldwide, the British Government in acknowledgement of Iqbal's literary accomplishments awarded him knighthood in 1922.[10]

## The role of Muslims in the advancement of Britain

During a debate on 'Islam' at the House of Lords on 19 November 2013, Baroness Warsi PC, the first Muslim to serve in a British cabinet, remarked:

> The fact is, British Muslims play a crucial role in British society. Everyone in this house knows Muslims in British life – doctors, engineers, scientists, journalists, MPs, teachers, business people, local councillors and so on. They are all making strong contributions to our country... The first recorded Englishman to become Muslim was John Nelson, in the 16th century. At the time of the union with Scotland in 1707, Muslims were already in Britain. There are records of Sylhetis working in London restaurants as early as 1873. Noble Lords may also be aware of the recent campaign that the Government launched to highlight the contribution of the nations from the Commonwealth during the First World War. Hundreds of thousands of the 1.2 million who served in the British Indian Army were Muslims. They fought and died for the values and freedoms that we enjoy today.[11]

Following the Second World War, the population of working men in Great Britain decreased and there was a need for foreign workers in order to keep the country's economy moving. Hence, the British Government encouraged foreigners to come, work and settle in Great Britain. As a result, Muslims began to arrive in Great Britain along with followers of other religions. After 1960, the influx of Muslim immigrants increased significantly resulting in the population of Muslims reaching hundreds of thousands. In Great Britain today, the population of Muslims is the largest after that of the Christians.

Together we have all contributed to the development of Great Britain. A small example will assist us in truly considering the collective advancement and progress made. When I came to Great Britain in 1974, there was only one complete motorway, the M1, and a journey from London to Birmingham via the A40 would take hours. However, today there is a web of motorways covering the whole country. These motorways were built and maintained by the contributions of the citizens of this country by virtue of taxation including the road tax for instance, and in this we are all equally a part. Furthermore, according to a recent survey conducted by ICM Research UK, Muslims are the top charity givers and donors in Great Britain, and their charity is benefitting those in need nationally and internationally.

## The role of Muslims in British politics

In Great Britain, the Muslims have played their role in all walks of life including employment, education, health, charity, business, armed forces, police etc. and they have also played their part in politics. They are engaged in service from being local councillors to becoming Members of Parliament, Lords and Ministers of Government.

Prominent names of Muslim politicians include Lord Nazir

Ahmed (Rotherham), Baroness Sayeeda Warsi (Dewsbury), Mohammad Sarwar (Glasgow) and Sadiq Khan (London) among others. In particular, Lord Nazir Ahmed has become a bold and accepted voice for Muslims around the world, and not only in Britain.

## The population of Britain

Great Britain is a multi-cultural, multi-racial and multi-religious country. According to the 2011 Census, the total population of the United Kingdom was about 63,705,000 and from this, the population of Great Britain was about 61,894,137. In terms of religion, the largest population was of the Christians followed by the Muslims, who constituted 5% of the total population and other communities, such as Hindus, Sikhs, Jews, Buddhists, etc., together formed 4% of the total population. Only in England and Wales, the population of Muslims was 2.7 million and the population of other religions excluding the Christians was 2.1 million.

## The laws of Britain and the laws of Islam

As a whole, the British society is peaceful, helpful, well-mannered and broad-minded. Most people think positive, however there are always individuals of a negative mind within every society and every religious community.

In my estimate, probably about thirty percent, at most, of the laws and norms of this country are contrary to Islam. For example, limitless freedom in speech, drinking of alcohol, consumption of pork, bodily exposure, man and woman living together without marriage and sex education in schools, etc. Furthermore, many of these matters are such that they are not forced upon every citizen, rather one can abstain from them. For example, if there are issues surrounding sex education in schools, etc., then alternatives are available in the form of Islamic schools and there is a need to further establish Islamic schools. Similarly, if an employee faces the issue of selling alcohol or pork at work, then although in a circumstance of need this is permissible for him, but if he wishes to be cautious then alternative employment can be sought.

However, more than seventy percent of the laws of this country are rather similar and in conformity with Islam, which Western intellectuals acquired from Muslim Spain. For example, upholding of justice, prevention of cruelty, recompense for the afflicted, importance of education, protection of wealth and person, religious freedom, child support and benefit, rights of the neighbours, human compassion and provision of the basic necessities of life such as food, clothing and a home, etc. These are rights enjoyed by each British citizen.

The humane principles adopted by the advanced and developed nations of the world today after centuries of experience, Islam demonstrated those principles in practice fourteen centuries ago. Just considering the provision of basic necessities of life, some examples of Islamic teachings are presented here:

1.  Our beloved Prophet Muhammad ﷺ stated, "The son of Adam has a right in three: a home wherein he may reside, clothing with which he may conceal his private parts, and a morsel of bread to consume."[12]

2.  'Umar ibn al-Khattab al-Faruq [ra] said, "If the kid of a goat, or a lamb dies on the far embankment of the River Euphrates out of negligence (hunger and thirst), I fear that Allah will call me to account for that."[13]

3.     One night, a commercial caravan laid camp close to the Prophetic Mosque. 'Umar al-Faruq [*ra*] said to 'Abd al-Rahman ibn 'Awf [*ra*], "Come, let us watch over this caravan tonight so that no-one steals their chattels." At that instance, 'Umar al-Faruq [*ra*] heard the crying sound of a child, and so they approached its mother and said, "Fear Allah, and silence him by cheering him up." A short while later, the child cried again, and so 'Umar al-Faruq [*ra*] again told his mother, "Cheer up your child." In the last portion of the night when the child cried again, 'Umar al-Faruq [*ra*] said to her strictly, "You are such a merciless mother. Why do you not cheer him up?" She replied, "O servant of Allah! You are pestering me for no reason. I am weaning him off milk because the Caliph 'Umar does not appoint (financial) benefits for children until they have stopped breastfeeding." Hearing this, 'Umar al-Faruq [*ra*] was shocked, and immediately after leading the morning prayer (*fajr*) congregation, he said, "Alas 'Umar! How many a child may you have killed," and he immediately had it announced, "Beware! Do not hasten the weaning of children off milk. After this day, financial benefits for the child shall be dispensed the day he is born."[14]

Today when some women place an allegation against Islam that Islam does not give women their rights, I request them to study the history of their gender. If they have not had the opportunity to read their history, let me present an aspect of their history here: In pre-Islamic days, a woman would not be allotted any share of inheritance, in any society of the world. In Europe, on one dying intestate, the eldest son of the deceased would inherit the total inheritance. This was known as 'primogeniture'. The widow, daughters and all other children would be deprived of any share of the inheritance. This very law prevailed in England till 1925, after which, instead of the eldest son, the widow would inherit the entire estate, which left the children at the mercy of the mother. Now, when this widow would marry again, there is a possibility that her second husband may prefer his own offspring and neglect the previous children of the woman. This would render dim the future for the previous children as they have already been denied inheritance. Anyhow, irrespective of whether the entire estate is given as inheritance to the primordial son or to the widow, it is utter injustice in either form. Highlighting the right to inheritance of women in Islam, HRH the Prince of Wales, Charles, stated:

> The rights of Muslim women to property and inheritance, to some protection if divorced, and to the conducting of business, were rights prescribed by the Qur'an fourteen hundred years ago... In Britain at least, some of these rights were novel even to my grandmother's generation.[15]

With the Arabs, it was customary for the adult sons, or brothers, of the deceased to inherit the entire property. The children, daughters and widow of the deceased would remain denied and the grounds put forth would be that those unable to prove their bravery in the battlefield and incapable of seizing the booty, they are undeserving of inheritance. Whereas the woman and the innocent young children were, in fact, more deserving to inheritance in order to fulfil their basic needs, but this oppression and brutality prevailed against them.[16]

Fourteen hundred years ago, on the face of the earth, Islam was the very first religion to declare women and children as inheritors. It allotted shares to each individual, according to their requirements, abolished the exclusiveness of the primordial son and thereby, rendered all heirs entitled to the heritage of their late father.

---

## Notes

1   *The New Encyclopaedia Britannica*, 15th edition (Chicago: Encyclopaedia Britannica, Inc., 1995), vol. 12, p. 141.
2   Nabil Matar, *Islam in Britain: 1558-1685* (New York: Cambridge University Press, 1998), pp. 10-11, 18, 28.
3   ibid., p. 34.
4   *Account* is the autobiography of Joseph Pitts (d. 1739) of Exeter, published in 1704.
5   Nabil Matar, *Islam in Britain: 1558-1685*, p. 38.
6   Ron Geaves, *Islam in Victorian Britain: The Life and Times of Abdullah Quilliam* (Markfield: Kube Publishing Ltd, 2010), p. 3.
7   <http://abdullahquilliam.com/wp/about-abdullah-quilliam> [accessed 4 February 2014]
8   Shaykh Muhammad Karam Shah al-Azhari, 'Iqbal's Concept of Love', *Maqalat* (Lahore: Zia-ul-Qur'an Publications, 1990), vol. 2, p. 49.
9   *Brief Life Sketch*. < http://www.allamaiqbal.com/person/perbrief.html> [accessed 20 February 2014]
10  Shaykh Abdul Qadir, 'Preface', *Kulliyyat-e Iqbal: Urdu* (Lahore: Maktaba Jamal, 2007), p. 14.
11  *Hansard: House of Lords*, Grand Committee Tuesday 19 November 2013. <http://www.publications.parliament.uk/pa/ld201314/ldhansrd/text/131119-gc0001.htm> [accessed 4 February 2014]
12  Al-Tirmidhi, *Sunan al-Tirmidhi* (Cairo: Thesaurus Islamicus Foundation, 2000), book of *al-zuhd* (32), chapter 30, hadith 2512.
13  Al-Hindi, *Kanz al-'Ummal fi Sunan al-Aqwal wa'l-Af'al* (Beirut: Mu'assasat al-Risalah, 1985), vol. 5, p. 756, hadith 14294; Abu Nu'aym, *Hilyat al-Awliya' wa Tabaqat al-Asfiya'* (Beirut: Dar al-Kutub al-'Ilmiyyah, 2002), vol. 1, p. 89, hadith 141.
14  Ibn Sa'd, *Kitab al-Tabaqat al-Kabir* (Cairo: Maktabat al-Khanji, 2001), vol. 3, p. 280; Ibn al-Jawzi, *Sirat wa Manaqib 'Umar ibn al-Khattab* (Cairo: Dar al-Taqwa li'l-Turath, 2000), p. 62; Muhammad Husayn Haykal, *al-Faruq 'Umar* (Cairo: Dar al-Ma'arif, 2006), vol. 2, p. 195.
15  H.R.H. The Prince of Wales, *Islam and the West*, a lecture given in the Sheldonian Theatre, Oxford, on 27 October 1993 (Oxford: Oxford Centre for Islamic Studies, 1993), p. 15.
16  Al-Qurtubi, *al-Jami' li Ahkam al-Qur'an* (Dar al-Kitab al-'Arabi), in the commentary of 4:7.

# CHAPTER 3

# I am a British Muslim

LET US PLACE the average Muslim immigrant to Great Britain in the first person of this conversation and then reflect:

> I came to Great Britain in search of a better livelihood. I worked well and hard and in doing so I contributed towards the strengthening of the British economy on the one hand, and by sending money back to my family on the other hand, I helped the economy of that country too. The economic progress, religious freedom, human compassion, opportunities for work, education, health, protection, justice and social security impressed me so much that I migrated to this country with my family and applied for the right of abode and indefinite leave to remain in the United Kingdom. Demonstrating generosity, Great Britain gave me and my family British nationality and citizenship and then the British passports.
>
> I am a British Muslim and Great Britain is my country and that of my offspring and coming generations. My relationship with Great Britain is exactly the same as that of any non-Muslim British citizen.

## British citizenship

The main forms of acquiring British citizenship is by birth in the United Kingdom to a parent who is a British citizen at the time of birth or a parent who is settled in the United Kingdom, or by naturalisation as a British citizen. The commitment of a British citizen is represented by the oath of allegiance and the pledge that is made at citizenship ceremonies following which naturalisation is given.

## My oath of allegiance

I [name] swear by Almighty God that on becoming a British citizen, I will be faithful and bear true allegiance to Her Majesty Queen Elizabeth the Second, her Heirs and Successors, according to law.[1]

## My pledge

I will give my loyalty to the United Kingdom and respect its rights and freedoms. I will uphold its democratic values. I will observe its laws faithfully and fulfil my duties and obligations as a British citizen.[2]

## My rights and responsibilities

While living temporarily or permanently in the United Kingdom, an individual has the right to:

- be treated fairly and lawfully regardless of his or her race, gender, age, religion, sexual orientation or any disability; and
- practise his or her own religion – similarly he or she is

expected to show respect for people of other faiths.[3]

While living temporarily or permanently in the United Kingdom, it is the responsibility of the individual to:

- obey the law;
- care for his or her children (for example, children under the age of 16 must always be supervised by an adult, and they must go to school if they are aged between five and 16); and
- report to the police, if he or she is required to do so.[4]

---

Notes

1   United Kingdom Border Agency, Home Office, section 'Citizenship ceremonies', <http://www.bia.homeoffice.gov.uk/britishcitizenship/applying/ceremony/> [accessed 7 February 2014]

2   ibid.

3   United Kingdom Border Agency, Home Office, section 'Rights and responsibilities', <http://www.ukba.homeoffice.gov.uk/visas-immigration/while-in-uk/rightsandresponsibilities/> [accessed 7 February 2014]

4   ibid.

# CHAPTER 4

# My responsibilities

As a British Muslim living in Great Britain and whilst enjoying the rights and provisions given to every citizen of this country, there are certain responsibilities and duties, based upon the teachings of Islam, that are to be observed.

## Adherence to the oath and pledge

Allah says:

يَـٰٓأَيُّهَا ٱلَّذِينَ ءَامَنُوٓا۟ أَوْفُوا۟ بِٱلْعُقُودِ

"O you who believe! Fulfil the obligations (promises)." (*Qur'an* 5:1)[1] In this verse, Allah has ordered the believers to fulfil every word given and every type of promise made, whether that is between the person and his Creator or between one person and another person, whether that is related to matters of religion or it concerns worldly affairs, and whether that undertaking is with a believer or with a non-Muslim. Fulfilling all promises is essential and adhering to them is an obligation.

The beloved Prophet Muhammad ﷺ said, "A hypocrite has three

signs: when he speaks he tells a lie, when he makes a promise he breaks it and when he is entrusted with something he cheats and defrauds."[2] The holy Prophet ﷺ further made it clear, "He who does not commit himself to his promise, he has no religion."[3]

The holy Prophet ﷺ was careful never to breach any promise or contract entered into with non-Muslims, polytheists, Jews or Christians; in fact, in addition to governmental covenants, the holy Prophet ﷺ was always careful to fulfil promises made on a personal and individual basis, as when Hudhayfah [ra] migrated from Makkah to Madinah, and the non-Muslims of Makkah captured him en route and hindered him from completing his journey. The reason given for this was that the non-Muslims were preparing to fight the Muslims and if Hudhayfah [ra] was allowed to continue his migration it would increase the number of Muslim soldiers. Hudhayfah [ra] stated, "Let me go on and leave me, for I promise that I will not participate in the fight against you." On the basis of this promise, the non-Muslims let him go. Eventually, when he arrived in Madinah, he informed the holy Prophet ﷺ of this whole incident. After some time, when the Battle of Badr was about to take place and the holy Prophet ﷺ commanded the Muslims to join in this battle, Hudhayfah [ra] also enlisted. When the holy Prophet ﷺ saw Hudhayfah [ra] amongst them, he stopped him taking part in the battle and stated, "Although we require every single individual, nevertheless, adhering to and fulfilling words and promises is essential."[4]

The 'Ulama' (scholars of Islam) reckon that this was a promise made under duress, in a state of powerlessness; Hudhayfah [ra] only gave his word to do away with them and therefore there was a case for breaking promises made under duress in a situation of war. Nonetheless, the holy Prophet ﷺ would not countenance breaking a promise to ensure that Muslims in future would not take this incident as an example or excuse to breach, betray or violate contracts and undertakings. Therefore, being a British Muslim, an individual must respect the oath of allegiance given to 'Her Majesty Queen Elizabeth the Second, her Heirs and Successors'.

One aspect of this agreement is that if a person is found breaking the law of this land or attempting to cause unrest, then attempts should be made to stop him from such violation of the country's laws and if after being given advice, the person does not mend his ways, then this should be brought to the attention of the authorities, because unrest and strife in this country will be detrimental for all citizens and their children.

It is absolutely correct that more than ninety percent of the Muslims in Great Britain are peaceful, however this fact can too not be ignored that amongst us there is a very small and limited minority in which tendencies of extremism and terrorism can be found. Therefore, it is our obligation that we collectively identify this extremist minority and address them through dialogue, and if we do not succeed then we ought to gain the assistance of the state authorities. However, it is our weakness that due to reasons of our own, such as social caste or close regional background, etc., we do not point out these radical elements. Although with regard to Islamic teachings we should not be falling into this shortcoming, for in the well-known saying of the holy Prophet ﷺ, he said that even if his daughter Fatimah was to commit theft, he would give her the deserving punishment of theft.[5] This is because the law is the same for all and all are equal in the eyes of the law.

The nation that conceals the black sheep within it and does not attempt to rectify or identify them, only a dark future awaits that nation. For how long shall we continue to announce our distance from incidents such as the 7/7 bombings, of 7 July 2005 in London, and the murder of Drummer Lee Rigby, of 22 May 2013 in Woolwich? The Government is exerting its effort, but we also need to become serious and genuine regarding this. If we do not take a practical step in the right direction today, then there is no point nor benefit in regret and disappointment tomorrow.

In relation to this, consider the following teachings of Islam:

1.  The holy Prophet ﷺ said, "Allah does not cause the common people to suffer punishment as a result of the particular people of sin. However, when they witness wrong among themselves and they do not protest against it whilst having the ability to do so, then Allah afflicts punishment upon the common people as well as those particular sinful criminals."[6] There are evil people in every age, however it is the collective responsibility of every nation that it does not conceal them, rather identifies them; it does not offer protection to criminals, rather brings them to justice; and it makes use of every means to discourage them. When a nation turns a blind eye to criminals, then slowly and gradually the entire nation becomes engulfed in crime and every individual's life becomes a torment.

2.  Al-Qurtubi has narrated a tradition that an angel was once instructed to destroy a certain community settlement. The angel asked, "But in this community lives that specific righteous worshipper?" The order came, "Then begin destruction from him, because never did his face change out of anger upon witnessing Our disobedience!"[7]

3.  The holy Prophet ﷺ said, "When the people witness an oppressor and do not take hold of his hands to prevent him from oppression, then very soon Allah will inflict punishment upon all of those people."[8]

4.  Whilst explaining this type of situation with a practical

example, once the holy Prophet ﷺ stated, "The example of those who firmly establish the limits of Allah and those who transgress them is like those people who drew lots to determine the seating arrangements on a boat. Thus, some of them were allotted seats on the upper deck and others were given space on the lower deck. When those who were on the lower deck wanted to drink some water, they had to pass through the people on the upper deck. So they said to one another that if they were to make a hole in the boat from the lower deck, then (they would attain water by ease and) they would not disturb the people on the upper deck with their continuous passing through. Now if those on the upper deck allowed these people to fulfil their intention on the lower deck, then (the full boat will be flooded with water and) all would drown and perish. And if those on the upper deck prevented the hands of these people from making a hole in the boat, then all of them on the upper deck and the lower deck will be saved."[9] This means that if a fragment of a nation and society is embarking upon a wrongful path and begins perpetrating such acts that would become the cause of destruction for the nation and the state, then it becomes the obligation of the responsible people of that society and nation, such as scholars, religious elders, political and cultural leaders, to put a stop to their endeavours, otherwise the entire nation and society would be rendered devastated and destroyed.

The statement of Albert Einstein is quite meaningful here, 'the world is a dangerous place to live; not because of the people who are evil, but because of the people who don't do anything about it;' as is the proverb attributed to Edmund Burke, 'evil prevails when good people fail to act.'

When an incident involving terrorism takes place, then one

terrorist rises and overwhelms the entire media hijacking all Muslims. Therefore, it is now necessary for the silent majority to speak, otherwise the consequence will not be good and people will continue to label us as terrorists.

## Appreciating the positives of the Government

The justice and fairness, peace and security, which the British Government has established in this country after continuous effort and determination, the Muslims ought to acknowledge and appreciate it with an open heart. Just as the beloved Prophet Muhammad ﷺ acknowledged and recognised the qualities of the Christian King al-Najashi (Negus).

When the holy Prophet ﷺ began preaching Islam in Makkah, the non-Muslims were severe in their opposition and made the lives of those people who accepted Islam unbearable. The oppression increased day by day. Then, the holy Prophet ﷺ gave his Companions permission to depart this locale of cruelty and barbarity and migrate to a land of honesty, Abyssinia, for the King there, al-Najashi, was known to be merciful and just; neither did he oppress anyone nor did he sanction the oppression of the weak. History records that al-Najashi did afford protection to the Muslims and forbade their oppression. Eventually, 'Uthman al-Ghani [ra], Ruqayyah [ra] the daughter of the holy Prophet ﷺ and Ja'far ibn Abi Talib [ra] together with others migrated to Abyssinia. The non-Muslims of Makkah sent a delegation to the King of Abyssinia asking him to expel the Muslims from his land, but when al-Najashi saw the reality of the situation he refused and sent the delegation back.[10]

By granting citizenship of this country, the British Government has provided each British Muslim the opportunity of benefitting from those provisions and facilities which were not available in the country of origin, nor are they available in any other Muslim country, otherwise one would not migrate and come here. If anyone is unable to accept this reality then he can find out for himself by traveling to any rich Muslim country he wishes and there file an application to gain the citizenship of that country. He will very soon feel the importance of Great Britain. Hence, it is a moral obligation that British Muslims acknowledge and appreciate the qualities and positives of this country and be grateful. For Allah says:

$$\text{هَلْ جَزَآءُ ٱلْإِحْسَٰنِ إِلَّا ٱلْإِحْسَٰنُ ۞}$$

"What is the response to good other than good?" (Qur'an 55:60)[11] Furthermore, the holy Prophet ﷺ said, "He who does not thank people cannot thank Allah."[12]

## The development of Britain

Great Britain is now the country and home of the children and coming generations of British Muslims too. Our children will benefit from its progress and development and our children will also suffer the consequences if it fails. Therefore, we ought to play our role in its development just as a Muslim would play his role in the development of any Muslim country. To understand this, an example from the Qur'an concerning a Prophet is presented here.

Prophet Yusuf (Joseph [as]) was sold as a slave in Egypt when he was eighteen years old and as a result of a false allegation he was imprisoned. When he had spent twelve years in prison, the King of Egypt had a dream which nobody was able to understand nor interpret. Prophet Yusuf [as] provided the interpretation of the King's dream that a severe drought was soon to strike Egypt, which would remain for seven years, therefore the King should appoint an honest minister of the state treasury who would be able to store corn and grain today so that the people could make use of it during the time of the impeding drought. The King responded, "Even if I gather all the people of Egypt together, they will not be able to fulfil this trust." At that time, Egypt was a non-Muslim land and its King was also not a Muslim, despite that, Prophet Yusuf [as] spoke out as mentioned in the words of the Qur'an:

$$ قَالَ ٱجْعَلْنِى عَلَىٰ خَزَآئِنِ ٱلْأَرْضِ إِنِّى حَفِيظٌ عَلِيمٌ ۝ $$

"He said, 'Appoint me (as minister) over the treasures of the land (of Egypt), indeed I am a good keeper, knowing well.'" (Qur'an 12:55)[13]

That non-Muslim King appointed Prophet Yusuf [as] as the State Treasurer. During the period of drought, Prophet Yusuf [as] created such a profound atmosphere by his effective planning and insight, and his justice and fairness, that eventually he was appointed the King of Egypt. Just as Prophet Yusuf [as] utilising all his capabilities served the non-Muslim populace of Egypt, as a result of which he became the ruler of Egypt, similarly if we were to make full use of our strengths and abilities in Great Britain, we can too surely gain important positions in this country. For democracy has matured here and whoever has the potential to move forward, there is nothing to prevent him.

## Respect towards others

British Muslims must respect the religion and culture of other people. If we want to win the respect of the Christians, Jews, and Hindus, etc., then we must respect them. As the beloved Prophet Muhammad ﷺ said, "None of you can become a (true) believer until he loves for all people what he loves for himself."[14]

The Qur'an offers clear guidance that whoever deals with you with respect, you should deal with him with even greater respect or at least show him equal respect. Allah says:

$$\text{وَإِذَا حُيِّيتُم بِتَحِيَّةٍ فَحَيُّواْ بِأَحْسَنَ مِنْهَآ أَوْ رُدُّوهَآ ۗ}$$
$$\text{إِنَّ ٱللَّهَ كَانَ عَلَىٰ كُلِّ شَىْءٍ حَسِيبًا ۝}$$

"And when you are greeted with a greeting, greet with a better (greeting) than it or (at least) return the same. Surely Allah takes account of all things." (*Qur'an* 4:86)[15] Furthermore, the Qur'an has encouraged respectful and just dealings with non-Muslims and it has announced the glad tidings of Allah's acceptance to those Muslims who opt for a just and pleasant mode of conduct with non-Muslims. Allah says:

$$\text{لَّا يَنْهَىٰكُمُ ٱللَّهُ عَنِ ٱلَّذِينَ لَمْ يُقَٰتِلُوكُمْ فِى ٱلدِّينِ وَلَمْ يُخْرِجُوكُم مِّن دِيَٰرِكُمْ أَن}$$
$$\text{تَبَرُّوهُمْ وَتُقْسِطُوٓاْ إِلَيْهِمْ ۚ إِنَّ ٱللَّهَ يُحِبُّ ٱلْمُقْسِطِينَ ۝}$$

"Allah does not forbid you regarding those who did not fight you in the matter of religion, nor drove you out of your homes, that you show them kindness and deal with them justly. Surely Allah loves those who do justice." (*Qur'an* 60:8)[16] The Qur'an has also prohibited actions that might become obstacles on the path of mutual respect. Allah says:

$$\text{وَلَا تَسُبُّواْ ٱلَّذِينَ يَدْعُونَ مِن دُونِ ٱللَّهِ فَيَسُبُّواْ ٱللَّهَ عَدْوًۢا بِغَيْرِ عِلْمٍ ۗ}$$

"And (O believers) do not revile those whom they worship besides Allah, lest they revile Allah out of spite due to ignorance." (*Qur'an* 6:108)[17] In other words, do not swear at anyone's god so that they in return do not swear at yours. The holy Prophet ﷺ severely reprimanded people for swearing at or abusing even the parents of any person and declared it a cardinal sin, because when you swear at somebody's parents, he in retaliation will swear at yours.[18]

On the basis of this command of Allah, i.e. not to insult anyone's god, and taking in consideration the present reality of the world that has become a global village, it is fair to say in my opinion that 'I have full right to prove that my religion is right, but I have no need to prove that other religions are wrong.' There is a famous Urdu proverb: *apne madhhab ko choro nahi, dusre ke madhhab ko chero nahi* (don't abandon your own religion, and don't poke at anyone else's religion).

To make this easier and to broaden the understanding of this point, an example is presented here. Every person has certain qualities that others are pleased with as well as certain weaknesses that others do not like. However, when a group of five or six individuals of one faith or community get together at some joyous or sorrowful occasion and they begin to remember the parents or forefathers of one another, they do not make mention of the faults and blemishes of any of their parents, rather they mention the qualities and positives and in doing so spend their time in a pleasant atmosphere. If they were to point out the faults of anyone's parents or forefathers, then unpleasantness and hatred takes over the atmosphere and sometimes the scene quickly turns to abuse and slander, quarrel and tussle, and in the long run even ending up in murder and killing.

In the same manner, every religion has certain positives that followers of other religions are pleased with and it also has certain beliefs and dogmas that others object to and differ with. Hence, in a society where people of different religions live together, they should keep their matters of difference within themselves or within the bounds of their own communities, and only those aspects and matters should be mentioned in society that are mutual and acceptable to all. For example, if in any circumstance a Jew, Muslim, Christian, Hindu, Sikh and an atheist are together and each one of them in turn mentions the qualities of his religion or belief, then none of the others would be offended because for each person, his own religion and creed is most dear and it is his right to express its qualities. However, quarrel only begins when a person insults and offends the religion of another.

Therefore, in a multi-religious society, every person has the right to praise his religion, but nobody has the right to insult or cause offence to any other religion. An African proverb states, 'if you damage the character of another, you damage your own.' Another famous proverb is quite straightforward concerning respect, 'give respect to gain respect.'

Once when the holy Prophet ﷺ was sitting together with his Companions, the coffin of a Jew was carried by. The holy Prophet ﷺ stood up and followed him with his eyes sadly. One of his Companions said, "He was a Jew," and the holy Prophet ﷺ replied, "Was he not human?"[19]

## Mutual understanding

British Muslims should learn about the faiths and cultures of other people and make them aware of Islam in order that they comprehend one another's values, and by discussing mutually shared values, they attain mutual confidence and reliance. For the Qur'an has encouraged acting upon and paying attention to mutually shared values. Allah says:

قُلْ يَٰٓأَهْلَ ٱلْكِتَٰبِ تَعَالَوْاْ إِلَىٰ كَلِمَةٍ سَوَآءٍۭ بَيْنَنَا وَبَيْنَكُمْ

"Say (dear Prophet), 'O People of the Book! Come to a word common between us and you.'" (*Qur'an* 3:64)[20] Therefore, rather than propagating conflicts and disputes by focussing on controversial issues, attempts should be made to make the atmosphere more pleasant by stressing commonly shared values and making them the topic of discussion.

Where there is mutual understanding, mutual confidence and respect will automatically prosper. Albert Einstein famously made a statement that 'peace cannot be kept by force, it can only be achieved by understanding.'

## Tolerance and liberal mindedness

British Muslims must refrain from statements liable to cause sorrow or distress to anyone, and if anyone makes a comment that saddens them, then they should try to tolerate it as much as possible following the teachings of Islam. As Allah says:

وَلَا تَسْتَوِى ٱلْحَسَنَةُ وَلَا ٱلسَّيِّئَةُ ٱدْفَعْ بِٱلَّتِى هِىَ أَحْسَنُ فَإِذَا ٱلَّذِى بَيْنَكَ وَبَيْنَهُۥ عَدَٰوَةٌ كَأَنَّهُۥ وَلِىٌّ حَمِيمٌ ۝

"Good and evil are not equal. Repel the evil with good; that is better. Thus the person between whom and you there is enmity he will become as your intimate friend." (*Qur'an* 41:34)[21]

Occasionally, there are heated arguments between husband and wife, however it is tolerated by both of them because each is aware that they have to live together. In exactly the same manner, harsh comments made by others should be tolerated as far as possible because we all have to live in this country together. Thereafter, when we tolerate their behaviour reciprocally they will tolerate ours. In this way, an atmosphere of peace and tranquillity will flourish that shall benefit the whole society in general.

In this respect, remember the action of the beloved Prophet Muhammad ﷺ. A delegation from the Christians of Najran came to Madinah with the objective of debating with the holy Prophet ﷺ regarding Prophet 'Isa (Jesus [as]). When this delegation reached the Prophet's Mosque, the holy Prophet ﷺ had just finished the mid-afternoon prayer ('asr). The Christians entered the mosque and began worshipping facing the east. Some of the Companions sought to hinder them, but the holy Prophet ﷺ deterred them. Thus they worshipped with full comfort and satisfaction according to their beliefs and practices inside the Prophet's Mosque.[22]

---

## Notes

1   *Qur'an, Surat al-Ma'idah* (chapter 5), verse 1.

2   Al-Bukhari, *Sahih al-Bukhari* (Cairo: Thesaurus Islamicus Foundation, 2000), book of *al-iman* (2), chapter 25, hadith 33.

3   Ahmad, *Musnad Ahmad ibn Hanbal* (Istanbul: Dar al-Da'wah, 1982), vol. 3, p. 135.

4   Muslim, *Sahih Muslim* (Cairo: Thesaurus Islamicus Foundation, 2000), book of *al-jihad* (33), chapter 35, hadith 4740.

5   Al-Bukhari, *Sahih al-Bukhari*, book of *ahadith al-anbiya'* (60), chapter 57, hadith 3514.

6   Ahmad, *Musnad Ahmad ibn Hanbal*, vol. 4, p. 192.

7   Al-Qurtubi, *al-Jami' li Ahkam al-Qur'an* (Dar al-Kitab al-'Arabi), in the commentary of 5:63; Ibn Hayyan, *al-Bahr al-Muhit fi'l-Tafsir* (Beirut: Dar al-Fikr, 1992), in the commentary of 5:63.

8   Al-Tirmidhi, *Sunan al-Tirmidhi* (Cairo: Thesaurus Islamicus Foundation, 2000), book of *al-fitan* (29), chapter 8, hadith 2321.

9   Al-Bukhari, *Sahih al-Bukhari*, book of *al-sharikah* (47), chapter 6, hadith 2534.

10  Ibn Hisham, *al-Sirah al-Nabawiyyah* (Beirut: Dar al-Jil, 1975), vol. 1, p. 280; Shaykh Muhammad Karam Shah al-Azhari, *Sirat Diya' al-Nabi* (Lahore: Zia-ul-Qur'an Publications), vol. 2, p. 343.

11  *Qur'an, Surat al-Rahman* (chapter 55), verse 60.

12  Ahmad, *Musnad Ahmad ibn Hanbal*, vol. 4, p. 278.

13  *Qur'an, Surat Yusuf* (chapter 12), verse 55.

14  Ahmad, *Musnad Ahmad ibn Hanbal*, vol. 3, p. 272.

15  *Qur'an, Surat al-Nisa'* (chapter 4), verse 86.

16  *Qur'an, Surat al-Mumtahinah* (chapter 60), verse 8.

17  *Qur'an, Surat al-An'am* (chapter 6), verse 108.

18  Al-Bukhari, *Sahih al-Bukhari*, book of *al-adab* (78), chapter 4, hadith 6039.
19  Al-Bukhari, *Sahih al-Bukhari*, book of *al-jana'iz* (23), chapter 49, hadith 1324.
20  *Qur'an, Surat Al 'Imran* (chapter 3), verse 64.
21  *Qur'an, Surat Ha Mim al-Sajdah* (chapter 41), verse 34.
22  Shaykh Muhammad Karam Shah al-Azhari, *Sirat Diya' al-Nabi*, vol. 4, p. 651.

# CHAPTER 5

# My neighbours

ISLAM IS A religion that seeks the peace and harmony of all people, hence it places great emphasis on the society and the relation between all segments within the society. It is for this reason that Islam has given specific importance and great significance to the concept of neighbours and the dealings between them upon which the success of the whole society depends.

The closest of neighbours to us are those families or individuals who reside to the left and right sides of our homes; the boundaries of their houses and gardens are adjacent to ours. These are the people we see many times every day. Sometimes they exit their homes and we see them from our windows when we are seated in our front rooms and sometimes they stroll in their gardens and are thus visible to us from our bedroom windows. When we exit our homes or lounge in our gardens, we often see one another, and therefore, they become a part of our daily lives.

Our neighbours are often aware of any work taking place in our homes or gardens and hence, they are, somewhat, confidants of ours.

In the unfortunate event – God forbid – of a fire in our house or if a terrorist attacked it, the first people to become aware of such an incident would be our immediate neighbours. If they are infuriated with us, then they may be glad to see us harmed, and it is likely that they would not attend to our rescue, and we would lose our lives. If, on the other hand, they are pleased with us, they would alert the police and the fire brigade, they would come to as much of our aid as they can, and it is quite possible for our lives to be saved by virtue of their efforts.

Cordial relations with neighbours, therefore, are the priority of every human being, so that we may come to the aid of one another in times of tragedy. In fact, I would not hesitate to go as far as stating that we should have acquaintance with the neighbour's pet dog so that it would not terrorise us with its barking.

## Exchanging gifts with the neighbours

1.  Abu Dharr [ra] reported that the beloved Prophet Muhammad ﷺ counselled him, "Whenever you cook soup, add some extra water into it in consideration for your neighbours, and give some of that soup to them out of the expression of good conduct."[1]

2.  A goat was slaughtered at the home of 'Abdullah ibn 'Amr [ra], and he twice asked his family, "Have you sent, or not, a gift of meat to our neighbour, who is a Jew, for I have heard the holy Prophet ﷺ saying, 'Jibril has always been advising me with regards to the neighbour, such that I began to believe that he would render the neighbour my inheritor.'"[2]

One manner of maintaining cordial ties with neighbours is via the exchange of gifts. When exchanging gifts, the parties must respect the religious sentiments of one another, and any such gift must not be made that may be disliked in the religion of the recipient.

## The good treatment of neighbours

1.  The beloved Prophet Muhammad ﷺ said, "According to Allah, the best neighbour is he who treats his own neighbour well."[3]

2.  The holy Prophet ﷺ said, "Whoever believes in Allah and the Day of Judgement, he should respect his neighbours."[4]

3.  Abu Dharr [ra] narrates that surely Allah loves that individual who, though his neighbour is ill-mannered and causes distress to him, he himself bears patience upon his afflictions.[5]

## Annoying the neighbours

1.  The beloved Prophet Muhammad ﷺ said, "By Him in Whose divine hands my life is! That individual will not enter Paradise from the mischief of whom his neighbour is not safe."[6]

2.  The holy Prophet ﷺ was asked, "Such-and-such a woman offers prayers during the night and she fasts during the day but she abuses her neighbours with her vituperation." The holy Prophet ﷺ said, "There is no goodness in her; she will go to Hell."[7]

Just imagine the value of neighbours in Islam, that the prayers and fasting of that woman will not save her from Hell who merely insults her neighbours with her tongue, and, moreover, how terrifying will be the consequence of that individual who inflicts physical harm upon them.

## Partaking in the sorrow and joy of the neighbours

Mu'awiyah [*ra*] once asked the beloved Prophet Muhammad ﷺ, "What right has my neighbour over me?"

To this, the holy Prophet ﷺ replied, "If he falls ill, pay him a visit; if he dies, attend his funeral; if he seeks a loan from you, give it to him; if he has a blemish, conceal it; if he receives any goodness, congratulate him; if calamity befalls him, commiserate with him; and do not raise the structure of your home higher than the structure of his home when that may prevent airflow to his home."[8]

By partaking in the sorrows and joys of neighbours, and by exchanging views with them, both parties become aware of the cultures and values of one another, and an environment of mutual understanding and trust is created. On the other hand, if contact is not maintained with the neighbour, then many misunderstandings may crop up unnecessarily, that may, eventually, lead to confusion and differences.

## We are all neighbours of one another

A neighbour is not only the one who resides adjacent to our home. To be precise, those people are also our neighbours who sit beside us in buses, planes, schools and mosques, and it is imperative for us to implement a noble conduct with them in order so that whatever time we spend there, it is spent well.

Likewise, if we observe from a broader angle then the residents of one street are the neighbours of the residents of the next street, the inhabitants of one city are the neighbours of the city next to it and the populace of one country are the neighbours of the populace of the neighbouring country. In effect, the world has assumed the profile of a global village, and therefore, all of the people of the world are neighbours of one another. If we respect the rights of all these neighbours, then nobody in the world would have to face oppression and tyranny.

## Eliminating malice and starvation from the world

1.  The beloved Prophet Muhammad ﷺ said, "By Allah, he is not a true believer! By Allah, he is not a true believer! By Allah, he is not a true believer!" The holy Prophet ﷺ was asked, "O Messenger of Allah! Who?" The holy Prophet ﷺ replied, "He from whose mischief his neighbour is not safe."[9]

2.  The holy Prophet ﷺ said, "He is not a true believer who eats satiated whilst his neighbour sleeps hungry."[10]

If every person of the world promises that, from this day onwards, he will not annoy his neighbour, and that every night, prior to retiring to bed, he will redress his grievances as much as he possibly can, then merely by applying these two concise prophetic traditions, the world can today transform into such a pleasant and pleasurable place wherein every individual would be delighted and content.

## Neighbourly conduct brings a non-Muslim to Islam

Observe the following event, as a token of blessings from the previous prophetic narration mentioned above: A few years ago, I watched the interview of a young man who previously was a non-Muslim. He told his story in the following manner:

> I had gone to Delhi to take an examination for BSE. In the room next to mine was a Muslim student who had also arrived to take the BSE examination. One day, I suffered an intense fever and I could not leave

my room the whole of that day, and nor could I visit the canteen to eat. That night, there was a knock on my door. With extreme difficulty, I managed to open the door, and I saw that in front of me was standing the Muslim student from next door. He said that he had not seen me outside that day, and nor in the canteen, and hence he had come to check on me so that he could help me. I told him, "You have done well. I have a strong fever. Please bring for me some medicine and some food from the shops."

At late night, he went out to the shops and brought medicine and food for me from afar. I thanked him and he went away to his room. I was relieved by the medicine and the food, and so therefore I was able to sit the examination on the following day. That Muslim captured my heart; had he not come to my support, I would have been unable to sit the examination. When the examination was over, I entered that Muslim's room and I said, "Do you know that I am a non-Muslim? I have no friendship with you, then why did you pay so much attention to me?"

The Muslim replied, "To be quite honest, it is the teaching of my religion that if any Muslim is about to go to bed on a full stomach when his neighbour is hungry, then he is not a good Muslim. Hence, to practise upon the teachings of my religion, I helped you." Hearing this, I began saying, "That religion which teaches empathy even with non-Muslims, I accept that religion." and so I became Muslim.

If each and every Muslim had been a practical Muslim like that young Muslim student in Delhi, then the image of Islam would have been quite different in the world today.

## The family of God

Not humankind and fellow citizens alone, Islam teaches us to be caring towards all of creation. The beloved Prophet Muhammad ﷺ said, "The entire creation is the family of Allah, and Allah loves him the most who treats His family well and benefits it the most."[11]

Thus, all creatures are the family of Allah, be they living or inorganic, human or animal, Muslim or non-Muslim; indeed the whole environment and each entity within it is a member of the family of Allah, and Allah loves whoever treats it well. There is no doubt that Allah would be displeased with whoever oppresses any member of His family.

---

## Notes

1 Muslim, *Sahih Muslim* (Cairo: Thesaurus Islamicus Foundation, 2000), book of *al-birr wa'l-silah wa'l-adab* (46), chapter 42, hadith 6855.

2 Al-Tirmidhi, *Sunan al-Tirmidhi* (Cairo: Thesaurus Islamicus Foundation, 2000), book of *al-birr wa'l-silah* (23), chapter 28, hadith 2069.

3 ibid., hadith 2070.

4 Al-Bukhari, *Sahih al-Bukhari* (Cairo: Thesaurus Islamicus Foundation, 2000), book of *al-adab* (78), chapter 31, hadith 6087.

5 Al-Hindi, *Kanz al-'Ummal fi Sunan al-Aqwal wa'l-Af'al* (Beirut: Mu'assasat al-Risalah, 1985), vol. 9, p. 51, hadith 24893.

6 Ahmad, *Musnad Ahmad ibn Hanbal* (Istanbul: Dar al-Da'wah, 1982), vol. 3, p. 154.

7 Al-Hakim, *al-Mustadrak 'ala'l-Sahihayn* (Beirut: Dar al-Kutub al-'Ilmiyyah, 1990), vol. 4, p. 184, hadith 7304; Ahmad, *Musnad Ahmad ibn Hanbal*, vol. 2, p. 440.

8 Al-Tabarani, *al-Mu'jam al-Kabir* (Baghdad: Matba'at al-Ummah, 1983), vol. 19, p. 419.

9 Al-Bukhari, *Sahih al-Bukhari*, book of *al-adab* (78), chapter 29, hadith 6084.

10 Al-Tabrizi, *Mishkat al-Masabih* (Beirut: Dar al-Fikr, 1991), book of *al-adab*, chapter of *al-shafaqah wa'l-rahmah 'ala'l-khalq* (15), section 3, hadith 4991.

11 Al-Bayhaqi, *Shu'ab al-Iman* (Beirut: Dar al-Kutub al-'Ilmiyyah, 1990), vol. 6, p. 43, hadith 7446; al-Tabrizi, *Mishkat al-Masabih*, book of *al-adab*, chapter 15, section 3, hadith 4999.

# CHAPTER 6

# My children

EARLIER IN THE chapter 'I am a British Muslim', it has been mentioned that as British citizens, it is our responsibility to care for our children, for example, children under the age of sixteen must always be supervised by an adult, and they must go to school if they are aged between five and sixteen. This guideline has two parts: supervision of children and education at school.

## Supervision of children

The supervision of children under the age of sixteen years is our responsibility so that no one causes physical, mental or spiritual harm to our children and we can nurture them so well that they too do not become the cause of someone else's physical, mental or spiritual harm.

The notion of supervising children has also been highlighted in the instruction of the beloved Prophet Muhammad ﷺ, in particular during the hours of darkness, when he stated, "Do not allow your animals and your children to go outside after sunset, for the devils spread after the sun has set."[1]

It is my experience that up to the age of sixteen, the children who have been provided with a moderate Islamic atmosphere at home and the Islamic beliefs are firmly and effectively embedded in their hearts and minds at the mosque, then moderate Islam imprints itself firmly on eighty or ninety percent of their mind and conscience that it becomes second nature to them. Thereafter, no wrongful society at college or university can turn them into extremists and terrorists. On the other hand, those children who do not enjoy a moderate Islamic atmosphere at home and the Islamic beliefs are not firmly established in their hearts and minds at the mosque, then eighty or ninety percent of their mind and conscience is left empty which can be filled by the wrongful society at college or university turning them into extremists. There exist many examples of this.

Therefore, we should not place the burden of our own weaknesses at home and in the mosque upon the college and university, rather we ought to make the system of education and nurturing at home and in the mosque so effective and dynamic that there is no space left in the minds and consciences of the children in which evil and extremism can enter. The proverbial statement of Desiderius Erasmus, 'prevention is better than cure,' has clear meaning and when the time has elapsed, it is no use crying over spilt milk.

## Education at school

Sending children to school from the age of five to sixteen years is the responsibility of parents or guardians. In terms of education, these eleven years of a person's life are very significant and important. At the age of sixteen, children sit their GCSE examinations and these examinations form the foundation of their educational future. If acceptable grades are achieved at the GCSE level, then A Levels and the company of an intellectual student society and atmosphere can be hoped for as well as a good degree, better livelihood and an eventual positive British citizen.

If, however, acceptable grades are not achieved at the GCSE level, then a basic course at college somewhat becomes an option as well as the company of silly individuals with negative minds, negative outcomes and in the end negative actions lead astray. Then we become concerned and worried at the waywardness of our children. However, we ought to think about why our children could not achieve acceptable grades at the GCSE level. If children from the Chinese and Indian ethnic backgrounds can attain a pass rate between sixty and eighty percent and the pass rate is less than forty percent for those of Pakistani origin as an example, then the school cannot be blamed, rather we are ourselves responsible. Therefore, rather than grieving over the failure of our children, we should grieve over our own weakness and deeply reflect upon the following sentences:

- Those who criticise the new generation, forget who raised it.
- Discipline your kids before they discipline you.
- Your children are your diamonds, look after them more than you care for your pounds.

Another statement deserving of being taken into consideration states, 'if we do not plant knowledge when young, it will give us no shade when we are old.'

## Islamic education

Allah says:

يَـٰٓأَيُّهَا ٱلَّذِينَ ءَامَنُوا۟ قُوٓا۟ أَنفُسَكُمْ وَأَهْلِيكُمْ نَارًا

"O you who believe! Save yourselves and your families from Hellfire." (*Qur'an* 66:6)[2] When this verse was revealed, 'Umar [*ra*] asked in all humility, "We can understand how we need to save ourselves from the fire of Hell, but how can we save our families?" The beloved Prophet Muhammad ﷺ replied, "Command them to do what is good and deter them from doing what is bad."[3]

Thus, it is the duty of parents to improve themselves by acting according to Islam's teachings and thereby ensure the proper moral and religious formation of their children.

## Scientific and technological education

If a student from India or Pakistan comes to study in Great Britain, he needs to travel a distance of thousands of miles, added to which there are student fees, residence, food and stationery costs. However, in Great Britain our children can get the same education virtually free and without travelling. Nonetheless, seventy-five percent of Muslim youth are achieving unacceptable grades at the GCSE level and are then becoming a burden on the state by falling victim to theft, unemployment, drugs and other crimes. Consequently, the Muslim prisoner population is exceeding in comparison to people of other faiths. Our children are lagging behind non-Muslims in scientific and technological education.

Thus, it is the responsibility of parents to encourage their children to pursue scientific and technological education, as well as education in religion. Just as our ancestors put Europe on the path of progress and advancement during the Middle Ages, so we too must play a role today in Britain's economic development.

## The first school

The first school a child enrols in is his mother's lap. It is this school that every child attends for the first four or five years of his life and from here the good and the bad of the child begins to develop. Some contend that during the first four or five years the intellectual ability of the children does not develop in such a way as to acquire a moral awareness, but this is a dubious contention. Normally, a child begins to speak at the age of two or three and by the age of four or five, every child is able to speak his or her mother tongue fluently.

A man of mature years like myself, if he were to begin learning the German language today, in two to three years time, he would not be able to speak German so fluently as a child speaks his mother tongue at the age of four or five years. Ponder the case of a child who can learn a language by just listening to it from the mother, so how can he not be affected by the good or bad character of the mother? Those parents who wish to teach their children their mother tongue, they speak in this tongue in their presence from the start. However, when telling a lie or acting unjustly toward others, parents forget that hearing lies and witnessing injustices likewise influence their children.

The daily life of the parent is a full-time silent teacher, from whom children are always learning. In front of children it is better to refrain from telling a lie even as a joke. Mothers and fathers should follow the etiquettes determined by Islam whilst speaking and in their manners, so that children may be encouraged to adopt Islamic values.

## The role of Imams and scholars

One duty of the Islamic scholars is to encourage children to refrain from all manner of bad behaviour such as quarrelling, violence, abusive language, law-breaking, theft, lying, drugs, etc. and to inspire them to perform good deeds such as acquiring knowledge, being truthful, behaving in a respectful manner, and so on.

In this country where the family system is crumbling and falling apart, the scholars in particular must teach children that Allah's pleasure depends on the pleasure of the father; if the father becomes angry, Allah will become angry,[4] and, as the beloved Prophet Muhammad ﷺ said, "Paradise is beneath the feet of the mother".[5] This is so that children respect their parents and the home atmosphere remains pleasant and peaceful.

This is also the teaching of the Bible, "Honour your father and mother, that you may have a long, good life in the land the Lord your God will give you." (Exodus, 20:12)[6]

On the other hand, one duty of the parents is that they must create the respect of the scholars and Imams within the hearts of the children. This is to ensure that they regard the scholars highly, thus, be affected by their teachings. As a result, they will learn the golden principles of Islam and respect their parents. Conversely, when children reach the age of maturity, parents should respect their thoughts and opinions as well. Through mutual understanding and logical argument, they should mutually resolve the issues they face.

## Friends of the children

Although a husband and wife have deep love for one another, nevertheless they do desire to have some sincere friends outside of the household with whom they can meet once or twice a month, have a meal together, whether by visiting their friends' home or inviting them over to their home, and spend some time talking in detail and discussing matters of mutual interest, and to seek benefit from the experiences of one another and also help each other during times of joy and sorrow. In the same manner, although children have deep love for their parents and siblings, nevertheless boys do wish to have friends from among the boys of similar age and girls do wish to have friends from among the girls of similar age with whom they can meet now and then, talk about things of mutual interest, have a meal together and play together.

Now just as parents select good clothes, a good school and a good teacher for their children, similarly it is their responsibility that they establish friendly relations with such people who themselves are good and their children are also good so that the friendship of their children and their company is with those who are good. If children at primary age of seven and eight years establish good friends then at the challenging atmosphere of secondary school, they will not be in need of searching for new friends. If parents do not assist in providing good friends for their children, then children will themselves make friends and if they select wrong friends and are led astray, then parents have no right to complain of their children for they did not fulfil their own responsibility.

## The Muslim family

The home is the foundational unit of any society and it is a critically important enterprise in Islam which directly affects the lives of those within the household as well as the development of all members of the family. Hence, Islam has encouraged that both husband and wife, whilst maintaining each one's role and responsibility, develop this segment of society into an ideal society for the betterment of themselves, their children and the wider community.

The husband and the wife are both human beings and there are no two such human beings in the world whose personalities and temperaments are one hundred percent the same. When the lines on the thumbs of two individuals do not match, then how can their dispositions be expected to be the same? Thus, when two people are always living together, it is natural for them now and then to have differences. Differences can sometimes lead to anger, but when this anger is not controlled, it can turn into harsh arguments and aggression that can lead to complete destruction of the home society, to the detriment of all members of the household and family. Differences should be discussed with mutual respect, love and compromise.

This is important as the relationship between husband and wife has a direct influence on the nurturing of the children. Normally it can be seen that the home in which a loving and respectful relationship is maintained between the husband and wife, the children being raised in that home tend to be civilised and obedient to the parents. Whereas, the home in which quarrel is the norm between the husband and wife, their children tend to be troublesome and disobedient.

---

## Notes

1   Muslim, *Sahih Muslim* (Cairo: Thesaurus Islamicus Foundation, 2000), book of *al-ashribah* (37), chapter 12, hadith 5372.
2   *Qur'an, Surat al-Tahrim* (chapter 66), verse 6.
3   Al-Qurtubi, *al-Jami' li Ahkam al-Qur'an* (Dar al-Kitab al-'Arabi), in the commentary of 66:6.
4   Al-Tirmidhi, *Sunan al-Tirmidhi* (Cairo: Thesaurus Islamicus Foundation, 2000), book of *al-birr wa'l-silah* (23), chapter 3, hadith 2020.
5   Al-Nasa'i, *Sunan al-Nasa'i* (Cairo: Thesaurus Islamicus Foundation, 2000), book of *al-jihad* (25), chapter 6, hadith 3117.
6   *The Living Bible*, British Edition (Eastbourne: Coverdale House Publishers Ltd, 1975), Exodus 20:12.

# CHAPTER 7

# My rights

ACCORDING TO THE law of Great Britain, a Muslim British citizen has the same rights and provision of facilities and services as any non-Muslim British citizen. For instance, if late at night – God forbid – our house catches fire, or it suffers a burglary, or we fall ill, then as a result of dialling 999, the fire brigade, police, ambulance and paramedic would be present at our doorstep readily providing every possible assistance to us. In our countries of origin, a commoner cannot at all even imagine such facilities and services. Therefore, we are proud over these conveniences and amenities.

However, there are certain laws and norms, the endless freedom of which has affected the rights and state of peace of British Muslims. At the top of the list is the law of freedom of speech which has paralysed our sense of religious freedom.

## The limits of freedom of speech

In accordance with the law of Great Britain, we enjoy religious freedom. However, the absolute and limitless freedom of expression has caused this blessing of religious freedom to suffer great difficulty and strain. Adolf Hitler was responsible for the

Holocaust physically killing six million Jews. On the other hand, individuals such as Salman Rushdie and Geert Wilders are responsible for killing the sentiments of more than one and a half billion Muslims by insulting the Qur'an and the bearer of the Qur'an, the beloved Prophet Muhammad ﷺ. The life of the one physically killed comes to an end, but the one whose sentiments have been killed, well he resembles a walking corpse; his heart, mind and soul remain restless and distressed. Freedom of speech has caused us to suffer the painful torment of a slow death.

Great Britain is our home and that of our children and coming generations. Great Britain is dear to us and we adhere to the laws of Great Britain. Therefore, it is our right that the British Government protects us from any form of mental anguish. For we are always apprehensive that at any moment any individual, relying on the freedom of speech claim, will suddenly launch a drone attack on Islam and then the British Government will suddenly come into action spending thousands of pounds only to shield and defend the attacker, but it will abandon the thousands of victims of this attack, like us, in an ocean of lament and protest without any helper nor sympathiser. It is indeed strange that there is no financial benefit for someone in insulting Islam and no harm will come to him if he refrains from such an action, despite that if he simply causes trouble by insulting Islam to express his own envy and hatred and to cause offence and worry for the Muslims, then to defend and shelter such a person and his action is, in my opinion, a waste of governmental resources and it is a kin to the mass killing of the emotions of a large segment of the population.

Therefore, the British Government should review the law on freedom of speech and by the freedom of one person's speech, it should not place hundreds of thousands of citizens in emotional stress and anxiety. Nonetheless, we respect the right to freedom of speech and expression but up to the limit where this freedom does not infringe and overstep the freedom of others. What freedom of speech is it that due to the behaviour of one individual, one and a half billion Muslims lose their sleep and chaos, destruction and killing erupts in different countries and parts of the world?

In this regard, a statement of the beloved Prophet Muhammad ﷺ is worthy of attention in which he instructed one of his Companions, Mu'adh ibn Jabal [ra], saying, "Love for other people what you desire for yourself, and detest for them what you hate for yourself, and speak of good or remain quiet."[1] This means that a person should speak of such matters in which there is good and remaining quiet is better than speaking of such matters in which there is evil and malice.

## An unbiased media

In the contemporary age, the media is the most powerful and effective means of creating and developing the mind-sets and attitudes of people. It is the genuine responsibility of the media that it portrays the qualities of the population and the government in such a light that the people in whom those qualities exist, they feel appreciated and valued, and the people who do not possess those qualities, they are encouraged to adopt them so that the population remains secure and the country progresses further.

The other responsibility of the media is that it highlights the failings and flaws of the population and the government in such a manner that the people in whom those faults exist, they are discouraged and begin focusing on rectifying them. However, it is important that the media does not express a deficiency or a failing in a manner that creates discord and dissention among the population.

Having said that, more than often we have seen that the media has not maintained this necessary balance. For example, when non-

Muslim British people comment against the Afghanistan or Iraq wars or against the country's foreign policy, their loyalty is not doubted and their view is accepted on the basis of a difference in opinion. However, when British Muslims comment or express these same views, a question mark is suddenly placed on their loyalty and allegiance. This is unfair and a discrimination against Muslims.

The British media must acknowledge and fathom the fact that Muslims, for being British, are loyal and devoted to Great Britain. They have the right to differ with any policy of the country and their view must also be accepted on the basis of a difference in opinion; and based upon this Islam as a religion must not be defamed and slandered. The British media is our media and we consider it our right to have a complaint and objection against it that when an extremist commits wrong in the name of Islam, ninety-five percent of the Muslim population condemns it, however the media highlights an interview of another extremist thereby concealing the opinion of the greater overwhelming majority and placing the rest of the people in a state of doubt and qualm regarding Islam. In this way, the media upsets and distresses hundreds of thousands of moderate and peaceful British citizens merely because of a handful of extremists.

## Anti-Islamic hate

The recent past has seen an increase in negative sentiments as well as crimes perpetrated which stem from anti-Islamic and anti-Muslim hatred. The neologism 'Islamophobia' is increasingly in use to reflect a strong feeling of dislike of Muslims, prejudice against them, hatred towards them as well as fear of them. On 27 December 2013, Tomas Jivanda in *The Independent* wrote:

Islamophobic hate crimes across Britain have risen

dramatically this year, new figures have revealed. Hundreds of offences were perpetrated against the country's Muslim population in 2013, with the Metropolitan police alone – Britain's largest force – recording 500 Islamophobic crimes, compared with 336 incidents in 2012 and 318 in 2011... However of the 43 forces, just 24 provided figures on the number of anti-Muslim crimes and incidents recorded – with some forces admitting they do not always record the faith of a religious hate crime victim. It is therefore likely that the actual numbers of incidents of hate crime against Muslims perpetrated in 2013 was much higher.[2]

This is indeed a reality which time and again comes to the forefront and creates difficulties and fears for the Muslims. The British Government, therefore, should accept this ground reality and just as the Jewish community is accorded protection through law and anti-Semitic behaviour is recognised, similarly it should also recognise and address the increase of Islamophobia and offer the Muslim community some form of protection and safeguards.

## Security of person and property

Despite being British citizens and adhering to the British laws, discrimination on the grounds of Islam does take place and appears in subtle forms. Moreover, individuals, their properties and organisations become victims of crimes against them. When children at school and women with headscarves and veils are targeted or when a pig's head is hurled at the mosque and Muslim centre of worship, it is the Muslim community and the Islamic faith that is targeted.

It is the right of every citizen that he, his property and his religion is given adequate protection. Those who spread terror in the community creating fear and dissention and those who perpetrate crimes based upon religious grounds, their punishment in law should be reviewed and increased so that this new wave of hatred and crime does not gather momentum and no one is left able to commit terrorism and crimes in the name of any religion.

## I am not a terrorist

Our religion is Islam and Islam is a religion of peace and security; there is no room for terrorism of any kind in it. Allah says:

$$مَن قَتَلَ نَفْسًا بِغَيْرِ نَفْسٍ أَوْ فَسَادٍ فِي ٱلْأَرْضِ فَكَأَنَّمَا قَتَلَ ٱلنَّاسَ جَمِيعًا وَمَنْ$$
$$أَحْيَاهَا فَكَأَنَّمَآ أَحْيَا ٱلنَّاسَ جَمِيعًا$$

"If anyone killed a person, other than for murder or (a punishment) for corruption on earth, it would be as if he killed all the people. And if anyone saved a life it would be as if he saved the lives of all people." (*Qur'an* 5:32)[3] This means that the killing and murder of any person (whether Muslim or non-Muslim) at the hands of any individual or any government without any reason or justification is equal to the killing and murder of all people. For the one who does not honour and respect any life is the enemy and foe of all humanity.

No individual has the right to decide on his own accord to kill someone else. In spite of this, if an individual takes the law of the land into his own hands even in the name of Islam, then he is a terrorist and he has no relation nor connection with Islam. Just as in every religion of the world there are people who are extremists and terrorists, similarly there are such people amongst the Muslims too. However, to label an entire religion as terrorism on the basis of these few criminals is complete unfairness and sheer injustice. HRH the Prince of Wales, Charles, stated:

> Our judgement of Islam has been grossly distorted by taking the extremes to be the norm. That is a serious mistake. It is like judging the quality of life in Britain by the existence of murder and rape, child abuse and drug addiction. The extremes exist, and they must be dealt with. But when used as a basis to judge a society, they lead to distortion and unfairness.[4]

Notes

1 Ahmad, *Musnad Ahmad ibn Hanbal* (Istanbul: Dar al-Da'wah, 1982), vol. 5, p. 247.

2 Tomas Jivanda, 'Islamophobia: Surge revealed in anti-Muslim hate crimes', *The Independent*, 27 December 2013. < http://www.independent.co.uk/news/uk/crime/islamophobia-surge-revealed-in-antimuslim-hate-crimes-9026873.html> [accessed 9 February 2014]

3 *Qur'an, Surat al-Ma'idah* (chapter 5), verse 32.

4 H.R.H. The Prince of Wales, *Islam and the West*, a lecture given in the Sheldonian Theatre, Oxford, on 27 October 1993 (Oxford: Oxford Centre for Islamic Studies, 1993), p. 14.

# CHAPTER 8

# Understanding Islam

ISLAM IS A complete code of life and a religion firmly in the hearts of one sixth of the world's population. It has a rich history that has contributed to the world we enjoy today. Its teachings stem from the holy book, Qur'an, and the life of the beloved Prophet Muhammad 쐹, transmitted from generation to generation through a vast array of disciplines and intellectual scholarship over the course of fourteen centuries. There is urgent need for Muslims and non-Muslims to develop an understanding of this religion. Due to prejudice, lack of understanding and open hatred of Islam as well as due to the un-Islamic behaviour of a small minority of Muslims, certain teachings of Islam are grossly being misrepresented and distorted. This has led to confusion in the world.

## Misreading the Qur'an

The holy book of the Muslims is the Qur'an revealed by Allah to the beloved Prophet Muhammad 쐹 over fourteen hundred years ago. It was revealed in the Arabic Language and even today its text is intact, unchanged and preserved as the very first day. It deals with every aspect of our lives, its teachings are comprehensive, sound, perfect and a source of pure guidance. The Qur'an is not merely written on paper, but in practice every word of the Qur'an has been transformed into action over the ages; it created a permanent civilisation and was a pivotal source of energy for reformation and intellectual as well as scientific pursuits resulting in the progress and advancement the world enjoys today.

History is witness that the Qur'an and its teachings changed a nation and that nation then inspired and changed the course of a greater part of the world.

Historically, the only enemies of the Muslims at first were the people of Makkah. But when the light of Islam began spreading in all four directions from Madinah, then many other tribes and states became occupied in attempting to wipe the Muslims off the face of the earth. In this way, the last eight or nine years of the life of the holy Prophet ﷺ were spent in warfare. Thus, the teachings revealed in this period should be observed in this context. If these teachings and commandments are considered from a different angle and taken away from their original context, it would be an injustice to the Qur'an and a riddance of honesty and integrity.

Consider a passing comment here, Allah says:

يَـٰٓأَيُّهَا ٱلَّذِينَ ءَامَنُواْ لَا تَقْرَبُواْ ٱلصَّلَوٰةَ وَأَنتُمْ سُكَـٰرَىٰ

"O you who believe! Do not approach the prayer when you are intoxicated." (*Qur'an* 4:43)[1] Now, if someone who does not offer the prayer takes out the first part of the verse from the context and says that he does not perform the prayer because the Qur'an orders, 'do not approach the prayer,' then will the claim of this person be valid in any circumstance? Clearly not. This would be a great injustice towards the Qur'an.

In further clarifying this reality, observe the following two references; the first biblical and the second from the history of Great Britain:

1.  "Don't imagine that I came to bring peace to the earth! No, rather, a sword. I have come to set a man against his father, and a daughter against her mother, and a daughter-in-law against her mother-in-law – a man's worst enemies will be right in his own home!" (Matthew, 10:34-36)[2]

2.  When Neville Chamberlain, Prime Minister of Great Britain, resigned on 10 May 1940, the leader of the all-party government, Winston Churchill, on 13 May 1940, in the House of Commons, London, said, "I have nothing to offer but blood, toil, tears and sweat. You ask, what is our policy? I will say: It is to wage war, by sea, land and air, with all our might. You ask, what is our aim? I can answer in one word: Victory – victory at all costs, victory, however long and hard the road may be."[3]

By observing these two excerpts at first sight, it could be assumed that Prophet 'Isa (Jesus [as]) and Winston Churchill were both despots and terrorists. However, the reality is not this. Since, when considered in light of the context of the two quotes, they both were clearly in complete accordance with the needs and demands of that time. Prophet 'Isa [as] was cautioning the individuals amongst his people that if they do not abandon their false beliefs, then they will have to face the separation of their close relatives who had accepted the truth. Winston Churchill was declaring war against Germany.

Similarly, the following two verses from the Bible, if they are also taken out of their original context, it would result in a different interpretation too:

1.    "The Lord is a man of war." (Exodus, 15:3)[4]

2.    "The Lord hath sworn that the Lord will have war with Amalek from generation to generation." (Exodus, 17:16)[5]

Understanding this point, if verses of the Qur'an are taken out of context, their meaning can be altered and if certain verses are related to wartime, then they should be viewed in light of this very context.

## The context of the beginning

The history of the battle between truth and falsehood is as old as the history of humankind. In order to rectify falsehood, truth has always made use of logical reasoning and permissible means, whereas in its opposition to truth, falsehood has always made use of obstinacy and impermissible power. The history of the Prophets is a clear proof of this reality.

For example, when our beloved Prophet Muhammad ﷺ raised the voice of truth, the entire town of Makkah gathered in enmity and opposition. The people who up until yesterday referred to him as the 'truthful' and the 'trustworthy', today had all of a sudden labelled him as a madman and magician. Moreover, whoever would accept Islam would be subject to mountains of cruelty and oppression. Sumayyah [ra] and Yasir [ra] were martyred in a cold and merciless manner and Bilal [ra] was physically tortured. When the Muslims had left Makkah and migrated to the land of Abyssinia, the people of Makkah sent a delegation to the King of Abyssinia to expel them from their land and in Makkah a conspiracy to murder the holy Prophet ﷺ was plotted. In short, after having had enough of the thirteen years of cruelty, the mercy to the world, the holy Prophet ﷺ, migrated from Makkah and arrived in Madinah. Even here, the people of Makkah did not allow the Muslims to sit in peace; rather, the Jews and the hypocrites were incited against the Muslims and in the second year following migration, with an army of one thousand, they marched on to Madinah to remove the Muslims from the face of the planet for good. At that moment, the mercy to the world, the holy Prophet ﷺ, with the permission of Allah raised the sword in defence accompanied by only three hundred and thirteen Companions.

It is astonishing that forces of enmity towards Islam do not see the first fifteen years of cruelty, they do not see the attack of one thousand non-Muslims from Makkah, however they straight away see these three hundred and thirteen compelled Muslims as they come out in their defence and so they say that these Muslims are quite some terrorists. Can any reasonable individual refer to this defence as terrorism?

## The state of the Arabs before Islam

When our beloved Prophet Muhammad ﷺ was born, at that time each Arab tribe would consider itself superior and would terrorise other tribes in order to maintain their control over them. If one person from the tribe was killed, the whole tribe would not rest until it had killed ten innocent persons from the other tribe in retaliation. In this way, year on year the process of violence and murder would continue amongst them. Some tribes of Arabia would bury their daughters alive so that no one becomes their son-in-laws. Just ponder, how would that mother sleep who knows that her daughter will be buried alive? Women and slaves were treated far worse than animals. The Qur'an has portrayed this in the following manner:

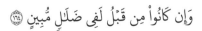

وَإِن كَانُوا۟ مِن قَبْلُ لَفِى ضَلَٰلٍ مُّبِينٍ ۝

"Whereas before this they were in manifest error." (*Qur'an* 3:164)[6]

$$ظَهَرَ ٱلْفَسَادُ فِى ٱلْبَرِّ وَٱلْبَحْرِ بِمَا كَسَبَتْ أَيْدِى ٱلنَّاسِ$$

"Corruption has appeared in the land and the sea because of what the acts of people have brought about." (*Qur'an* 30:41)[7] In other words, there was corruption in beliefs and corruption in deeds. No caravan travelling in the land was safe nor was any ship sailing in the sea. Rather, the fire of terrorism was burning everywhere. In order to put an end to this terrorism, Allah sent our beloved Prophet Muhammad ﷺ as an embodiment of mercy and ordered the people of Makkah indirectly:

$$فَٱذْكُرُوٓاْ ءَالَآءَ ٱللَّهِ وَلَا تَعْثَوْاْ فِى ٱلْأَرْضِ مُفْسِدِينَ ﴿٧٤﴾$$

"So remember the blessings of Allah and do not wander around in the earth spreading corruption." (*Qur'an* 7:74)[8]

## The holy Prophet's revolution

If one glances at the history of the world, then in the French Revolution and the Russian Revolution hundreds of thousands of people suffered and were affected adversely. Moreover, the pages of history of the world cannot at all ignore the horrid destructions of Nagasaki and Hiroshima. In this context, observe an overall analysis of the great revolution of the holy Prophet ﷺ:

The holy Prophet ﷺ tolerated the cruelty and barbarity of the non-Muslims for the first fourteen or fifteen years of his twenty three year era of Prophethood, and eventually left Makkah and migrated to Madinah, yet he did not raise the sword. However, in the second year following migration, when the Quraysh of Makkah mounted for an onslaught on the Muslims with an army of one thousand, then Allah permitted the Muslims to raise the sword in their defence. In this way, the last eight or nine years in the era of Prophethood were spent in battle. In these battles, the total number of fatalities was only one thousand and eighteen (1018) individuals from both groups, i.e. the Muslims and the non-Muslims.[9] The great revolution which Islam has given as a gift to humanity at a price of just this many human lives, its example cannot be found anywhere in the history of humankind.

Those tribes of Arabia, who were shedding rivers of blood of one another for centuries, they became such brothers that they were ready to die for one another. Those same people who were robbers and barbarians, they became peace-loving people and well-wishers of one another. Where caravans comprising of dozens of men would be robbed in broad daylight, there one woman on her own travels hundreds of miles and nobody would even harm her. Those Arabs who could not shepherd a few goats, they became leaders and guides of hundreds of thousands of people. This revolution not only changed the habits and customs of people, but it also affected and influenced future civilisations. The developed nations of the world today who take pride in the system of justice and fairness, equality and mannerisms, religious freedom, human rights, etc., the foundations for this system were provided by the Islamic revolution over fourteen hundred years ago.

The errors and wrongs to which the people of Arabia were victim before the Prophethood of the holy Prophet ﷺ and the revolution that occurred after his Prophethood, its brief introduction is presented in the words of Ja'far ibn Abi Talib [ra], which he presented to the King of Abyssinia when the ambassadors of Makkah were also present:

O King! We were an ignorant people. We worshipped

idols, consumed rotting animal flesh, committed all forms of indecency, ill-treated our relatives and neighbours and the powerful one among us would usurp the right of the poor. This was our state then Allah sent to us from amongst us such a Messenger whose ancestry we are well familiar with and whose truthfulness, trustworthiness and purity we are fully aware of. He has invited us to believe in Allah in the manner that we believe Him to be one and we only worship Him and that we leave the stones and idols which we and our forefathers used to worship. He has instructed us to speak the truth, not to cheat in trust, be good with the relatives, take care of the rights of the neighbours and refrain from wrong deeds and bloodshed. He has prohibited us from sinfulness and impiety, telling of lies, consuming the wealth of the orphans, accusing pure women of wrong and he has ordered to only worship Allah and not to associate any partner with Him, to establish the prayer, pay the prescribed alms and fast.[10]

Let us witness some glimpses of the unique life of this embodiment of mercy Prophet 鑾 who brought about the greatest and unrivalled revolution in the history of humankind:

## The holy Prophet's treaty as a young man

A leader of Makkah, namely Nabih ibn al-Hajjaj, was an oppressor and a terrorist. A Bedouin once visited the city of Makkah with his daughter. That terrorist abducted his daughter by force. That foreign Bedouin pleaded to the leaders of Makkah but they were themselves fearful of that abductor as he was very powerful as well as a tyrant. Every leader excused himself to the Bedouin stating his lack of audacity to protest against the abductor. The Bedouin was now sitting in a street of Makkah, crying. Thereupon, our beloved Prophet 翻, who was about nineteen years of age at the time, passed through that street and asked the depressed Bedouin, "Why are you sitting here so upset? What calamity has befallen you?" The Bedouin narrated his agonising story. The holy Prophet 翻 then said to him, "Go to the Ka'bah. I will be there shortly and I shall arrange some support for you."

The holy Prophet 翻 called out to his fellow youth to gather at the Ka'bah. The holy Prophet 翻 was famous amongst the people for being the 'truthful' and the 'trustworthy'; everyone respected him wholeheartedly; the children and the elderly, the men as well as the women. Within a few moments, all the youth of Makkah had gathered. The holy Prophet 翻 said to them, "This travelling Bedouin whom you see here, such-and-such a wealthy chieftain has forcibly abducted his daughter. It is incumbent upon us to redress his grievance." All the youths then said, "O Muhammad! Give us a command and we are ready to comply." The holy Prophet 翻 then stood them adjacent to the Ka'bah and administered to them an oath, "We swear that we will help the oppressed, and that we will not rest until the oppressed has been returned his right."

The holy Prophet 翻 took those youth, laid a siege around the house of that terrorist, and said to him, "We have come to have the daughter returned to the elderly Bedouin." Upon seeing the hot tempers of the youth, the leader replied that he needed a night to consider. The holy Prophet 翻 responded, "We cannot allow you a moment more. Either bring out his daughter or be prepared for a confrontation." Upon this, he immediately brought the daughter out. The holy Prophet 翻 submitted the girl to her father and said to him, "We shall accompany you to the outskirts of Makkah so that no one may cause harm to you."[11]

This incident is a glimpse of the character of that personality whom the forces of enmity towards Islam have had the audacity to accuse of terrorism.

This treaty of the youth was known as *hilf al-fudul*. Under the leadership of the holy Prophet ﷺ, the youth transformed the state and landscape of the entire city. Whenever any person would oppress another, the youth of *hilf al-fudul* would attend to his aid. Even after his declaration of Prophethood, our beloved Prophet ﷺ would narrate this treaty with pride and say, "If someone invites me to a similar treaty even today, I will gladly accept it." This tells us that if non-Muslims set up such organisations, then Muslims should also associate with them and play a fulfilling role against oppression and injustice. Since, tyranny and cruelty are detrimental for all human beings and it is the duty of every individual to struggle against them, whether he is a Muslim or a non-Muslim.

## The holy Prophet's conduct towards an enemy soldier

The holy Prophet ﷺ was returning with his army from the Battle of Dhat al-Riqa'. On the way they halted at a certain location and the entire army lied down to rest for a while in the shade of numerous trees. The holy Prophet ﷺ also hung his sword on a branch of a tree and rested. A soldier from the enemy ranks suddenly managed to secretly get to the holy Prophet ﷺ and, brandishing his sword, spoke out, "O Muhammad! Who can save you now from my sword?" The holy Prophet ﷺ replied, "My Allah will save me." Hearing this, spontaneously the soldier fell on his face down to the ground.

The holy Prophet ﷺ picked the soldier's sword up and said, "My Lord has saved me. Now you tell me, who will save you from my blow?" He replied, "No one can save me." The holy Prophet ﷺ

asked, "Do you accept Islam?" He replied, "That cannot be. However, I promise that I will never oppose you nor assist your enemy." Upon this, the holy Prophet ﷺ forgave him and returned his sword back to him. Witnessing this unique and unparalleled display of sublime character, the soldier spoke out, "Without a doubt! You are far better than me."[12]

Hearing the voice of the enemy soldier, the Muslim soldiers quickly gathered near the holy Prophet ﷺ. Now, ponder over the mercy and overlooking of the holy Prophet ﷺ. The enemy soldier had got very close to the holy Prophet ﷺ in order to martyr him and he had also rejected the invitation to accept Islam, if the holy Prophet ﷺ now wished, he could have easily killed him, yet he chose to forgive him.

## The holy Prophet's dealing with God's creation

When the people of Makkah breached the Treaty of Hudaybiyyah, the holy Prophet ﷺ set off from Madinah heading towards Makkah, in the year 8 AH, with an army of ten thousand. En route, the holy Prophet ﷺ saw a she-dog that had recently given birth to a litter of puppies who were suckling the milk of their mother. With this in mind that no soldier from the army (or the horse or camel of any soldier) harms them, the holy Prophet ﷺ appointed one of his Companions, namely Jamil ibn Suraqah [ra] to stand guard for the protection of that she-dog and its puppies, so that no soldier from the army of Islam would cause harm to that she-dog and its offspring."[13]

Just ponder, the Prophet who would not allow a she-dog to be scared and fearful, how can he perpetrate terrorism against the human beings? How unjust it is to refer to such a kind Prophet as a terrorist!

## Jihad (to struggle and strive)

*Jihad* (to struggle and strive) is a sacred obligation, however due to incorrect interpretation, it is being considered as corresponding to terrorism. Therefore, its comprehensive definition is necessary.

The literal meaning of the word *jihad* is 'to fully attempt and endeavour for something'.[14] In other words, it is to exhaust all energies of the heart and mind, knowledge and skill, wealth and soul and hand and tongue; in order to gain something or achieve some objective. This strive can be in the path of good, just as someone asked the holy Prophet ﷺ, "I intend to do *jihad?*" The holy Prophet ﷺ said, "Are your parents alive?" He replied in the affirmative, so the holy Prophet ﷺ said, "Do *jihad* in their service."[15]

This strive can also be in the path of evil, just as Allah says:

$$وَوَصَّيْنَا ٱلْإِنسَـٰنَ بِوَٰلِدَيْهِ حُسْنًا ۖ وَإِن جَـٰهَدَاكَ لِتُشْرِكَ بِى مَا لَيْسَ لَكَ بِهِۦ عِلْمٌ فَلَا تُطِعْهُمَآ$$

"And We have instructed each person to be good to his parents. But, if the parents strive to make you associate with Me that of which you have no knowledge, then do not obey them." (*Qur'an* 29:8)[16] In other words, although the parents are worthy of honour and respect, however when they endeavour to incline you towards polytheism (*shirk*) or evil, then they should not be obeyed. For this reason, the Qur'an has added the words *fi sabil Allah* (in the way of Allah) when mentioning the Islamic *jihad*,[17] to ensure that the passion of enmity, evil, lust for territorial control, worldly greed or personal desire do not enter into this *jihad* and only that *jihad* is meant in which the pleasure of Allah is central.

# Qital (to fight)

In pursuit of rectifying and bettering the condition, when all peaceful means become unsuccessful and injustice and oppression becomes unbearable, then in this circumstance armed *jihad* becomes necessary, which is referred to as *qital* (to fight) in Islamic terminology. The value of *qital* in Islam is the same as surgery in medical science i.e. the patient is only operated upon if all other non-surgical means and medicines have been tested and have failed.

## Struggle in the way of Allah

In Islam's Sacred Law (*shari'ah*), *jihad* refers to spending from the soul, wealth, tongue, etc., with full energy and struggle when fighting a battle in the way of Allah.[18]

In technical terminology, *jihad* refers to that struggle and strive which is pursued for Allah's sake; in the way of Allah, for Islam, for the governance of the community or for its stability; whether it is by means of wealth, soul or some other means.[19] It becomes clear from this that *jihad* is not simply the name for *qital*, rather every type of attempt for the stability of the nation has been labelled as *jihad*. To struggle and strive for knowledge and to spend on the stability and continuity of Islam from one's wealth are also *jihad*. Moreover, to speak the word of truth in front of a tyrant ruler is included within *jihad*. *Qital* is also part of *jihad* and this is its final and last possible form.[20]

## The beginning of fighting

The non-Muslims of Makkah subjected the Muslims to cruelty and barbarity for thirteen years, however the Muslims tolerated them with great patience. When, eventually, the Muslims migrated from Makkah to Madinah, even here there was no reduction in the injustices of the non-Muslims. Upon this, Allah granted the Muslims permission for *qital* (armed *jihad*) so that they can respond to the injustices and oppression of the non-Muslims with force.

If the occurrence of the first three battles between unbelief (*kufr*) and Islam and the number of Muslims is taken into consideration, the reality becomes absolutely clear that the non-Muslims and their allies attacked the Muslims in order to wipe them off the face of the earth and the Muslims raised the sword in order to defend themselves.

Take for instance, the Battle of Badr in the second year after migration, which was fought only ninety miles away from Madinah, in which the number of non-Muslims was one thousand and the number of Muslims was only three hundred and thirteen. The Battle of Uhud in the third year following migration was fought only a few miles away from Madinah, in which the number of non-Muslims was three thousand and the number of Muslims was only seven hundred. The Battle of Ahzab in the fifth year after migration was fought at the door of Madinah, in which the number of non-Muslims was ten thousand and the number of Muslims was only three thousand.

In view of these barbaric intents of the non-Muslims, Allah granted the Muslims permission to raise the sword.

## The etiquettes of fighting

Allah says:

وَقَـٰتِلُوا۟ فِى سَبِيلِ ٱللَّهِ ٱلَّذِينَ يُقَـٰتِلُونَكُمْ وَلَا تَعْتَدُوٓا۟ إِنَّ ٱللَّهَ لَا يُحِبُّ ٱلْمُعْتَدِينَ ﴿١٩٠﴾

"And fight in the way of Allah against those who fight you, and do not transgress the bounds. Indeed Allah does not love the transgressors." (*Qur'an* 2:190)[21]

In other words, if the circumstances of battle arrive, then the sword can only be raised against those who are partaking in the fight against you. Besides them, the killing of women, children, elderly and religious persons is not permissible. No dead body is to be mutilated. To the extent that animals, green fields and fruitful trees are not to be harmed unnecessarily.[22] This means that even in the heat of battle where passions and rage run wild and the fire of revenge burns fiercely, even there Islam bounds the fighters to justice and fairness, rules and regulations; so that no one is transgressed against and no one is treated unfairly because Allah does not like the transgressors.

Is there any such nation present in today's advanced and developed world who has taken care of the rule of law and justice and fairness in the heat of battle? Today, as soon as war commences, cities and populated lands are obliterated by bombings. Peaceful citizens, women, innocent children and the elderly are all not spared. Hospitals, places of worship and educational centres are all destroyed. Akbar Ilah Abadi has pointed towards this theme when he said:

> *They say that by the sword did Islam swell;*
> *By the canon what spread, they do not tell.*

This honour is only for Islam which even at the peak of battle where passions are uncontrollable, it does not allow for oppression against any innocent. If at the time, the Muslims were not granted permission to fight in their defence and to raise the banner of truth, then today the name of the Muslims would possibly not have existed in the world.

## Did Islam spread by the sword?

The people who accuse the holy Prophet Muhammad ﷺ of terrorism, one of their hypotheses is that the holy Prophet ﷺ used the activities of terrorism in order to promote and spread his religion. These people, in actual fact, are either ignorant of the initial thirteen-year history of Islam in Makkah or are guilty of deliberately concealing the facts and realities. Since, those men and women who accepted Islam in Makkah, they were not even granted permission to raise the sword in their defence against the oppression and cruelty they were being faced with. This was the reason for which they were compelled to eventually migrate from Makkah.

Can the objectors tell us that the sword came into the hands of the Muslims after migration, however those hundreds of Muslims who migrated from Makkah towards Madinah in the state whereby they were faced with utmost oppression, by the fear of whose sword did they accept Islam? At that time, the sword was not in the hands of the Muslims, rather it was in the hands of the non-Muslims of Makkah.

It is quite apparent that the sword as a result of whose force Islam spread, that sword was not made of metal, rather it was the sword of the beauteous character of the holy Prophet Muhammad ﷺ, as a result of which all of Arabia came into the folds of Islam within the span of a few years.

*It was a bolt of lightning, or the voice of a guide;*
*Which did all of a sudden shake the Arabian land.*

Islam respects religious freedom, just as Allah says:

$$\text{لَآ إِكْرَاهَ فِى ٱلدِّينِ}$$

"There is no compulsion in religion." (*Qur'an* 2:256)[23] If there was the permission of compulsion in religion then the day of the conquest of Makkah was a golden opportunity.

The persecutors who did not spare a single moment in harming and oppressing the holy Prophet ﷺ and the Muslims for up to twenty one years, they had all become overpowered on the day of the conquest of Makkah. They could have been forced to accept Islam. However, the mercy to the world, the holy Prophet ﷺ, forgave them and it was not a condition in this announcement of pardon that only those will be forgiven who accept Islam; rather, the announcement of pardon on that was such that whosoever drops his weapons, closes the door to his house, enters the house of Abu Sufyan or enters the mosque, he will be granted peace.[24]

It was the blessing of this practical example of the mercy to the world, the holy Prophet ﷺ, that no Muslim ruler in history has forcefully compelled any non-Muslim to accept Islam. If there was any room for this, then no non-Muslim would have remained during the rightly-guided caliphate (*khilafah rashidah*) and, similarly, there would have remained no Christian or Jew in Spain during the Middle Ages, and no Hindu in India during the Mughal era. All would have been forced to become Muslims, however this did not happen.

Islam is today progressing in the developed and advanced countries such as America and Europe. The original citizens of these lands are also accepting Islam. If Islam spread by the sword, then today the sword is with America and Europe, the Muslims have come here as labourers and subjects. Then what sword is attracting the original citizens of these lands towards Islam? It is clear that this is not the metal sword, rather it is the sword of the natural teachings of Islam which is attracting the sound mind and intellect towards itself.

Of all the battles that took place in the lifetime of the holy Prophet ﷺ, there is not a single one of them which was for the purpose of changing the religion of any nation or tribe. Furthermore, no nation alters its religion and faith out of fear of the sword or by way of greed of wealth. Even then if someone doubts this, then using the sword and wealth, he should demonstrate and test it, no nation will change its religion. Today, aside from the fifty or more Muslim countries, Muslims are also present in every other country, yet not a single one of them up until today has claimed that he was made a Muslim by means of force or greed.

To make someone a believer (*mu'min*) using the sword is not possible, because to become a believer simply uttering the affirmation by the tongue is not enough, rather the confirmation of the heart is also essential. If someone affirms Islam with his tongue but rejects it with his heart, then such a person is a hypocrite, whose state is worse than that of non-Muslims, because he can cause more damage and harm to Islam by remaining amongst the Muslims.

Who does not know that a sword by conquering a person's body and tongue can make him a hypocrite, but it cannot change the realm of the heart and make him a believer?

It is the beloved life of our beloved Prophet Muhammad ﷺ and the beloved teachings of our beloved Islam which are capturing the hearts of the people that whosoever truly accepts Islam once, then no greed of the world nor any severe persecution can distance him from Islam.

## The mercy to the world

Allah is Himself the utmost Kind and the ever Merciful. He sent our beloved Prophet Muhammad ﷺ as a complete embodiment of mercy. Allah says:

$$\text{وَمَآ أَرْسَلْنَٰكَ إِلَّا رَحْمَةً لِّلْعَٰلَمِينَ ۝}$$

"And We have sent you only as a mercy for all the worlds." (*Qur'an* 21:107)[25] All praise is for Allah, who is Lord of all the worlds and He is the One who sent our beloved Prophet Muhammad ﷺ as a mercy for all the worlds. In other words, to whatever Allah is Lord, to that the holy Prophet Muhammad ﷺ is mercy.

The mercy to the world, the holy Prophet ﷺ, is not only compassionate and merciful to the believers, rather he is also mercy for the non-Muslims. Similarly, he is not only a mercy for all the different types of people among the human race, rather his mercy spreads towards the animals, plants and birds.

Some brief details of this are as follows:

1.  Abu Hurayrah [*ra*] relates that the holy Prophet ﷺ said, "I am that mercy which Allah granted His creation as a gift."[26]

2.  Abu Umamah [*ra*] relates that the holy Prophet ﷺ said, "Allah has sent me as a mercy and guidance for all the worlds."[27]

## Mercy to non-Muslims

1.  Abu Hurayrah [*ra*] relates that the holy Prophet ﷺ was asked, "Pray against the polytheists." The holy Prophet ﷺ

replied, "I have not been sent as a curser, rather I have been sent as a mercy."[28]

2.    'A'ishah Siddiqah [ra], Mother of the Believers, relates that she asked the holy Prophet ﷺ, "Did a day more severe than the day of Uhud ever come upon you?" ... Mentioning the tribes of Ta'if, the holy Prophet ﷺ said that the angel of the mountains was sent to him saying, "If you instruct me, this entire dwelling (Ta'if) will be crushed between these mountains." However, the holy Prophet ﷺ said, "No. Rather, I am hopeful that Allah will create from their offspring such servants who will worship only Him and will not associate any partner with Him."[29]

## Mercy to women and servants

'A'ishah Siddiqah [ra] states that the holy Prophet ﷺ never struck anyone except in *jihad* in the way of Allah, never raised his hand on a woman and never struck any servant.[30]

## Mercy to animals

Prior to the advent of Islam, certain customs were present among the Arabs which were a means of causing pain to animals. For example, incising the flesh of a living animal or severing its tail, branding it, target-firing at it, etc. The holy Prophet ﷺ forbade all such acts and commanded compassion, mercy and good treatment to animals.

1.    Ibn 'Abbas [ra] relates that the holy Prophet ﷺ forbade the fighting and inciting of animals against one another,[31] as that causes suffering and harm to them.

2.    Shaddad ibn Aws [ra] relates that the holy Prophet ﷺ said,

"Allah has commanded noble treatment of all things, so therefore, whenever you kill, kill in the best manner, and when you slaughter, slaughter in the best manner. When one of you desires to slaughter, he should hone the knife and give relief to the slaughter animal."[32] This means that if one was to kill a dangerous animal, he should not cause it to suffer, but rather, it should be killed as swiftly as possible, and when one is to slaughter a lawful animal, it should be slaughtered with a sharp knife so that it suffers minimal pain. It is preferable not to sharpen the knife in the presence of the slaughter animal, and nor should any animal be slaughtered in view of another animal.

## Mercy to the camel

1.  Sahl ibn Hanzaliyyah [ra] relates that the holy Prophet ﷺ passed by a camel, the back of which was almost touching its belly. The holy Prophet ﷺ said, "With regards to these inarticulate animals, fear Allah! Mount them when they are mountable, and slaughter and eat them when they are edible."[33] In other words, when these animals suffer from hunger, thirst, pain or exhaustion, they are unable to inform you, so you yourself should take care of them, otherwise you will have to answer in the court of Allah.

2.  Anas ibn Malik [ra] reported that whenever they would dismount at a station, they would unload the litters off the camels prior to offering the prayer.[34] In Arabia, travelling would mostly take place during the night due to the excess of the heat of the day, and during the day, whenever the sun's heat would intensify, they would seek rest in the shades of trees. Hence, in the commentary of this *hadith*, al-Khattabi writes, "Whenever they would rest, they would primarily remove the litters off the camels, so that the camels could

feel at ease, and thereafter, the travellers would offer the midmorning prayer. It is preferable, with some scholars, that wherever the travellers take rest, they should feed silage to the animals prior to having food themselves. If any guest on a mount arrives, feed fodder to the horse prior to offering food to the rider."[35]

3. 'A'ishah [ra] mounted a restive camel and she began to gyrate it. The holy Prophet ﷺ said, "O 'A'ishah! Be gentle, as gentleness in anything makes the item beautiful, and whatever is devoid of gentleness, it becomes ugly."[36] Moreover, the holy Prophet ﷺ said, "O 'A'ishah! Allah is gentle, He loves gentleness and He bestows so much by virtue of gentleness of what He would not bestow by virtue of aggression or otherwise."[37]

## Mercy to the dog

1. Abu Hurayrah [ra] relates that the holy Prophet ﷺ said, "One hot day, a fornicatress (from the Israelites), saw a dog that had its tongue hanging out due to thirst, circling around a well. That woman filled her leather sock with water and gave it to the dog. By virtue of this noble deed, that woman was forgiven."[38]

2. The noble Companions asked, "O Allah's Messenger! Will we be rewarded for extending good treatment to animals?" The holy Prophet ﷺ replied, "There is reward in everything of moist liver (i.e. showing compassion to every living being)."[39]

## Mercy to the cat

'Abd Allah ibn 'Umar [ra] relates that the holy Prophet ﷺ said,

"One woman was punished and condemned to Hell because of a cat, as she had tied it up, and consequently, it died of starvation."[40] The Prophet who cannot tolerate the killing of a cat, how would it tolerate the killing of a human being!

## Mercy to birds

1.  Sa'id ibn Jubayr [ra] relates that 'Abdullah ibn 'Umar [ra] passed by a group of youth from the Quraysh, who, by way of sport, had suspended a bird and they were shooting arrows at it. When those youth saw 'Abdullah ibn 'Umar [ra], they dispersed. 'Abdullah ibn 'Umar [ra] said, "Whoever does this, i.e. use a bird for sport, Allah and His Messenger ﷺ have cursed him."[41]

2.  'Abdullah ibn 'Amr [ra] relates that the holy Prophet ﷺ said, "Whoever needlessly kills a sparrow, or a bird smaller than that, on the Day of Judgement, Allah will question him." The holy Prophet ﷺ was asked, "What is the right of birds?" The holy Prophet ﷺ replied, "It is the right of birds that they are slaughtered and eaten, and their head is not severed and cast away."[42]

3.  'Abdullah ibn Mas'ud [ra] relates: During one journey, we were with Allah's Messenger ﷺ. The holy Prophet ﷺ departed to answer the call of nature. Meanwhile, we captured two young birds from the offspring of a sparrow. The sparrow began to hover above our heads. When the holy Prophet ﷺ returned, he said, "Which one of you have caused distress to this sparrow by taking its young? Return them to the sparrow."[43]

4.  When the conqueror of Egypt, 'Amr ibn al-'As [ra], intended to travel to Alexandria from Cairo, he ordered his army to

take down his tent (*fustat*), but when he saw that a pigeon had laid eggs in the apex of the tent, he said, "This pigeon has sought refuge in our neighbourhood, therefore, so long as its young do not mature and fly away, this tent must not be taken down." Later, a city was established at that location, and it was named Fustat by virtue of that tent.[44]

## Mercy to the environment and vegetation

It is narrated from Anas [*ra*] that the beloved Prophet Muhammad ﷺ said, "Whatever the Muslim sows or plants, and birds, human beings and quadrupeds eat of it; that is rendered a charity on his behalf."[45]

Today, scientists have reached the conclusion that trees and verdant fields are imperative to maintain a healthy environment; however, our beloved Prophet ﷺ has encouraged this fourteen hundred years ago, so much so that every Muslim deems it his good fortune to partake in planting trees, as that shall be a continuous charity (*sadaqah jariyah*) after his demise. Moreover, human sympathy also calls for it, as it is narrated that one elderly man was planting a date palm tree when someone said to him, "You may have died by the time when this tree is able to bear fruit." He replied, "The ancestors before us planted trees and we ate their fruit. Now, it is our duty to plant trees so that the future generations may eat of their fruit."

The first caliph, Abu Bakr al-Siddiq [*ra*] sent an army towards Syria and instructed them, "Do not kill a woman, a child or an elder. Do not cut a fruit bearing tree. Do not destroy green and verdant fields. Do not slaughter a goat or a camel except for the need to eat only. Do not burn honeybees and do not disperse them."[46]

It is understood from this that, even in battle in the land of the enemy, Islam only permits to fight those soldiers who have come to fight them. Other than them, raising the sword towards their women, children and elders is not permitted nor is it permitted to slaughter their animals except for the need to eat, even to the extent that it is not permitted to destroy their trees and fields; because trees and fields are the needs of all people and, therefore, to waste them is enmity towards humanity itself which Islam does not allow.

## Ending note

It is the utmost extent of astonishment that today certain elements of the media, which bear hostility towards Islam, are attempting unsuccessfully to prove this Messenger of Mercy to be a terrorist, who was only sent to put an end to and rid the world of terrorism and misguidance. However, how has the media developed this daring audacity to label the Messenger of Peace as a terrorist? The reason for this is quite clear and is enshrined in the following couplet:

*Had we not forgotten the lesson of the Qur'an;*
*Time would not have shown the world, this time.*

*It is the decree, since eternity, of the judge of destiny;*
*Sudden demise is the price for the crime of frailty.*

---

### Notes

1 *Qur'an, Surat al-Nisa'* (chapter 4), verse 43.
2 *The Living Bible,* British Edition (Eastbourne: Coverdale House Publishers Ltd, 1975), Matthew 10:34-36.
3 David Ferriby and Jim McCabe, *Modern World History* (Oxford: Heinemann Educational Publishers, 2002), p. 123.
4 *The Holy Bible (Authorised King James Version),* Collins (London: Waverley Book Company Ltd, 1954), Exodus 15:3.

5  ibid., Exodus 17:16.

6  Qur'an, Surat Al 'Imran (chapter 3), verse 164.

7  Qur'an, Surat al-Rum (chapter 30), verse 41.

8  Qur'an, Surat al-A'raf (chapter 7), verse 74.

9  Shaykh Muhammad Karam Shah al-Azhari, Sirat Diya' al-Nabi (Lahore: Zia-ul-Qur'an Publications), vol. 7, p. 576.

10  Ahmad, Musnad Ahmad ibn Hanbal (Istanbul: Dar al-Da'wah, 1982), vol. 1, p. 202.

11  Al-Halabi, al-Sirah al-Halabiyyah (Beirut: Dar al-Kutub al-'Ilmiyyah, 2002), vol. 1, p. 192; Shaykh Muhammad Karam Shah al-Azhari, Sirat Diya' al-Nabi, vol. 2, p. 123.

12  Al-Alusi, Ruh al-Ma'ani fi Tafsir al-Qur'an al-'Azim wa'l-Sab' al-Mathani (Beirut: Dar al-Fikr, 1978), in the commentary of 4:102.

13  Al-Salihi, Subul al-Huda wa'l-Rashad fi Sirat Khayr al-'Ibad (Cairo: al-Majlis al-A'la li'l-Shu'un al-Islamiyyah, 1997), vol. 5, p. 322.

14  Al-Kasani, Bada'i' al-Sana'i' fi Tartib al-Shara'i' (Beirut: Dar al-Kutub al-'Ilmiyyah, 2003), vol. 9, p. 379.

15  Al-Bukhari, Sahih al-Bukhari (Cairo: Thesaurus Islamicus Foundation, 2000), book of al-adab (78), chapter 3, hadith 6038.

16  Qur'an, Surat al-'Ankabut (chapter 29), verse 8.

17  Qur'an, Surat al-Baqarah (chapter 2), verse 218.

18  Al-Kasani, Bada'i' al-Sana'i' fi Tartib al-Shara'i', vol. 9, p. 379.

19  Sayyid Qasim Mahmood, Islami Encyclopaedia, 8th edition (Lahore: Al-Faysal), vol. 1, pp. 744.

20  ibid.

21  Qur'an, Surat al-Baqarah (chapter 2), verse 190.

22  Malik, al-Muwatta' (Cairo: Thesaurus Islamicus Foundation, 2000), book of al-jihad (21), chapter 3.

23  Qur'an, Surat al-Baqarah (chapter 2), verse 256.

24  Al-Halabi, al-Sirah al-Halabiyyah, vol. 3, p. 115.

25  Qur'an, Surat al-Anbiya' (chapter 21), verse 107.

26  Al-Bayhaqi, Dala'il al-Nubuwwah wa Ma'rifat Ahwal Sahib al-Shari'ah (Beirut: Dar al-Kutub al-'Ilmiyyah, 2002), vol. 1, p. 158.

27  Ahmad, Musnad Ahmad ibn Hanbal, vol. 5, p. 257.

28  Muslim, Sahih Muslim (Cairo: Thesaurus Islamicus Foundation, 2000), book of al-birr wa'l-silah wa'l-adab (46), chapter 24, hadith 6778.

29  Al-Bukhari, Sahih al-Bukhari, book of bad' al-khalq (59), chapter 7, hadith 3267.

30  Muslim, Sahih Muslim, book of al-fada'il (44), chapter 20, hadith 6195.

31  Al-Tirmidhi, Sunan al-Tirmidhi (Cairo: Thesaurus Islamicus Foundation, 2000), book of al-jihad (19), chapter 30, hadith 1810.

32  Muslim, Sahih Muslim, book of al-sayd wa'l-dhaba'ih (35), chapter 11, hadith 5167.

33  Abu Dawud, Sunan Abi Dawud (Cairo: Thesaurus Islamicus Foundation, 2000), book of al-jihad (15), chapter 47, hadith 2550.

34  ibid., chapter 48, hadith 2553.

35  Al-'Adhimabadi, 'Awn al-Ma'bud Sharh Sunan Abi Dawud (Cairo: Dar al-Hadith, 2001), vol. 5, p. 52.

36  Muslim, Sahih Muslim, book of al-birr wa'l-silah wa'l-adab (46), chapter 23, hadith 6768.

37  ibid., hadith 6766.

38  ibid., book of al-salam (40), chapter 41, hadith 5998.

39  Al-Bukhari, *Sahih al-Bukhari*, book of *al-musaqat* (42), chapter 10, hadith 2403.

40  ibid., hadith 2405.

41  Muslim, *Sahih Muslim*, book of *al-sayd wa'l-dhaba'ih* (35), chapter 12, hadith 5173.

42  Al-Hindi, *Kanz al-'Ummal fi Sunan al-Aqwal wa'l-Af'al* ((Beirut: Mu'assasat al-Risalah, 1985), vol. 15, p. 37, hadith 39970.

43  Abu Dawud, *Sunan Abi Dawud*, book of *al-jihad* (15), chapter 122, hadith 2677.

44  Ibn al-Jawzi, *al-Muntazam fi Tawarikh al-Muluk wa'l-Umam* (Beirut: Dar al-Fikr, 1995), vol. 3, p. 194.

45  Al-Bukhari, *Sahih al-Bukhari*, book of *al-muzara'ah* (41), chapter 1, hadith 2361.

46  Malik, *al-Muwatta'*, book of *al-jihad* (21), chapter 3, hadith 971.

# Bibliography

*Qur'an*: the glorious revelation of Allah revealed to the final Messenger, the holy Prophet Muhammad 🕋.

*'Awn al-Ma'bud Sharh Sunan Abi Dawud*, al-Imam Abu'l-Tayyib Muhammad Shams al-Haqq Al-'Adhimabadi (d. 1319 AH), Cairo: Dar al-Hadith, 2001.

*Bada'i' al-Sana'i' fi Tartib al-Shara'i'*, al-Imam 'Ala' al-Din Abu Bakr ibn Mas'ud al-Kasani al-Hanafi (d. 587 AH), Beirut: Dar al-Kutub al-'Ilmiyyah, 2003.

*Al-Bahr al-Muhit fi'l-Tafsir*, al-Imam Muhammad ibn Yusuf ibn Hayyan al-Andalusi al-Gharnati (d. 754 AH), Beirut: Dar al-Fikr, 1992.

*Dala'il al-Nubuwwah wa Ma'rifat Ahwal Sahib al-Shari'ah*, al-Imam Abu Bakr Ahmad ibn al-Husayn ibn 'Ali al-Bayhaqi (d. 458 AH), Beirut: Dar al-Kutub al-'Ilmiyyah, 2002.

*Al-Faruq 'Umar*, Muhammad Husayn Haykal, Cairo: Dar al-Ma'arif, 2006.

*Hilyat al-Awliya' wa Tabaqat al-Asfiya'*, al-Imam al-Hafiz Abu Nu'aym Ahmad ibn 'Abdullah al-Asfahani al-Shafi'i (d. 430 AH), Beirut: Dar al-Kutub al-'Ilmiyyah, 2002.

*1001 Inventions: Muslim Heritage in Our World*, 2nd edition, ed. by Salim T S Al-Hassani, Manchester: Foundation for Science, Technology and Civilisation Ltd, 2007.

*Islam: A Profound Insight*, Ahmad M. Hemaya, Cairo: Zamzam Presses, 2011.

*Islam and the West*, H.R.H. The Prince of Wales, Oxford: Oxford Centre for Islamic Studies, 1993.

*Islam in Britain: 1558-1685*, Nabil Matar, New York: Cambridge University Press, 1998.

*Islam in Victorian Britain: The Life and Times of Abdullah Quilliam*, Ron Geaves, Markfield: Kube Publishing Ltd, 2010.

*Islami Encyclopaedia*, 8th edition, Sayyid Qasim Mahmood, Lahore: Al-Faysal.

*Al-Jami' li Ahkam al-Qur'an*, al-Imam Abu 'Abdullah Muhammad ibn Ahmad al-Ansari al-Qurtubi (d. 671 AH), Dar al-Kitab al-'Arabi.

*Kanz al-'Ummal fi Sunan al-Aqwal wa'l-Af'al*, 'Allamah 'Ala' al-Din 'Ali ibn Hisam al-Din al-Hindi (d. 975 AH), Beirut: Mu'assasat al-Risalah, 1985.

*Kitab al-Tabaqat al-Kabir*, Muhammad ibn Sa'd ibn Mani' al-Zuhri (d. 230 AH), Cairo: Maktabat al-Khaniji, 2001.

*Kulliyyat-e Iqbal: Urdu*, 'Preface', Shaykh Abdul Qadir, Lahore: Maktaba Jamal, 2007.

*Maqalat*, Justice Shaykh Muhammad Karam Shah al-Azhari (d. 1418 AH), Lahore: Zia-ul-Qur'an Publications, 1990.

*Mishkat al-Masabih*, al-Imam Muhammad ibn 'Abdullah al-Khatib al-Tabrizi (d. 741 AH), Beirut: Dar al-Fikr, 1991.

*Modern World History*, David Ferriby and Jim McCabe, Oxford: Heinemann Educational Publishers, 2002.

*Al-Mu'jam al-Kabir*, al-Hafiz Abu'l-Qasim Sulayman ibn Ahmad al-Tabarani (d. 360 AH), Baghdad: Matba'at al-Ummah, 1983.

*Al-Muntazam fi Tawarikh al-Muluk wa'l-Umam*, Jamal al-Din Abu'l-Faraj ibn 'Abd al-Rahman ibn al-Jawzi (d. 597 AH), Beirut: Dar al-Fikr, 1995.

*Musnad Ahmad ibn Hanbal*, al-Imam Ahmad ibn Hanbal (d. 241 AH), Istanbul: Dar al-Da'wah, 1982.

*Al-Mustadrak 'ala'l-Sahihayn*, al-Imam al-Hafiz Abu 'Abdullah Muhammad ibn 'Abdullah al-Hakim al-Naysaburi (d. 405 AH), Beirut: Dar al-Kutub al-'Ilmiyyah, 1990.

*Al-Muwatta'*, al-Imam Malik ibn Anas (d. 179 AH), Cairo: Thesaurus Islamicus Foundation, 2000.

*Ruh al-Ma'ani fi Tafsir al-Qur'an al-'Azim wa'l-Sab' al-Mathani*, al-Imam Abu'l-Fadl Shihab al-Din al-Sayyid Mahmud al-Alusi al-Baghdadi (d. 1270 AH), Beirut: Dar al-Fikr, 1978.

*Sahih al-Bukhari*, al-Imam Abu 'Abdullah Muhammad ibn Isma'il al-Bukhari (d. 256 AH), Cairo: Thesaurus Islamicus Foundation, 2000.

*Sahih Muslim*, al-Imam Muslim ibn al-Hajjaj al-Naysaburi (d. 261 AH), Cairo: Thesaurus Islamicus Foundation, 2000.

*Shu'ab al-Iman*, al-Imam Abu Bakr Ahmad ibn al-Husayn ibn 'Ali al-Bayhaqi (d. 458 AH), Beirut: Dar al-Kutub al-'Ilmiyyah, 1990.

*Al-Sirah al-Halabiyyah*, al-Imam Abu'l-Faraj Nur al-Din 'Ali ibn Ibrahim ibn Ahmad al-Halabi al-Shafi'i (d. 1044 AH), Beirut: Dar al-Kutub al-'Ilmiyyah, 2002.

*Al-Sirah al-Nabawiyyah*, al-Imam Abu Muhammad 'Abd al-Malik ibn Hisham (d. 213 AH), Beirut: Dar al-Jil, 1975.

*Sirat Diya' al-Nabi*, Justice Shaykh Muhammad Karam Shah al-Azhari (d. 1418 AH), Lahore: Zia-ul-Qur'an Publications.

*Sirat wa Manaqib 'Umar ibn al-Khattab*, Jamal al-Din Abu'l-Faraj ibn 'Abd al-Rahman ibn al-Jawzi (d. 597 AH), Cairo: Dar al-Taqwa li'l-Turath, 2000.

*Subul al-Huda wa'l-Rashad fi Sirat Khayr al-'Ibad*, al-Imam Muhammad ibn Yusuf al-Salihi al-Shami (d. 942 AH), Cairo: al-Majlis al-A'la li'l-Shu'un al-Islamiyyah, 1997.

*Sunan Abi Dawud*, al-Imam Sulayman ibn al-Ash'ath Abu Dawud al-Sijistani (d. 275 AH), Cairo: Thesaurus Islamicus Foundation, 2000.

*Sunan al-Nasa'i*, al-Imam Abu 'Abd al-Rahman Ahmad ibn Shu'ayb al-Khurasani al-Nasa'i (d. 303 AH), Cairo: Thesaurus Islamicus Foundation, 2000.

*Sunan al-Tirmidhi*, al-Imam Abu 'Isa Muhammad ibn 'Isa ibn Sawrah al-Tirmidhi (d. 279 AH), Cairo: Thesaurus Islamicus Foundation, 2000.

*The Holy Bible (Authorised King James Version)*, Collins, London: Waverley Book Company Ltd, 1954.

*The Living Bible*, British Edition, Eastbourne: Coverdale House Publishers Ltd, 1975.

*The New Encyclopaedia Britannica*, 15th edition, Chicago: Encyclopaedia Britannica, Inc., 1995.

*The New Universal Encyclopedia*, ed. by Sir John Hammerton and Gordon Stowell, London: The Caxton Publishing Company Limited.

# Author's other works

Titles of other works of the author, Muhammad Imdad Hussain Pirzada, published by Al-Karam Publications Ltd:

Works in English:

- *Tafsir Imdad al-Karam (commentary of the Qur'an, vol. 1)*
- *Muhammad; the Sublime Messenger* 🕮
- *Beloved Daughters of the Sublime Messenger* 🕮
- *Beloved Wives of the Sublime Messenger* 🕮
- *Reflections; a quest for answers to today's questions*
- *Human Rights; in light of the Qur'an and Sunnah*
- *Reality of the Film 'Innocence of Muslims' and Challenges of the Twenty First Century*
- *The Status of a Woman in Islam*
- *Muslims in a Multicultural Society*
- *Islamic Way of Worship*
- *Islam: the Complete Way of Life*
- *Imdad al-Sarf (Arabic Etymology)*
- *Imdad al-Nahw (Arabic Syntax)*
- *Islamic Beliefs*
- *The Beautiful Life of Muhammad* 🕮
- *The Ideal Mother; in light of the Qur'an, Sunnah and Tradition*

- *The Ideal Father; in light of the Qur'an, Sunnah and Tradition*

## Works in Arabic:

- *Imdad al-Fiqh fi'l-'Ibadat*
- *Imdad al-'Arabiyyah (Arabic Grammar Exercise Book)*
- *Al-Muntakhabat al-Imdadiyyah min al-Ahadith al-Mustafawiyyah*
- *Tafsir Surat al-Fatihah*

## Works in Urdu:

- *Tafsir Imdad al-Karam (commentary of the Qur'an, 5 vols)*
- *Islami Ibadat*
- *Islami 'Aqa'id*
- *Jamal-e Sirat al-Nabi* 
- *Awrat ka Maqam; Qur'an awr Sunnat ki rawshni mein*
- *Mithali Ma; Qur'an awr Sunnat ki rawshni mein*
- *Insan kay Huquq; Qur'an awr Sunnat ki rawshni mein*

## Works in English/Urdu:

- *The Fundamental Beliefs of Islam (Guldasta 'Aqa'id)*
- *Imdad al-Sarf (Arabic Etymology)*
- *Imdad al-Nahw (Arabic Syntax)*
- *Islam for Young Boys (Part 1)*
- *Islam for Young Boys (Part 2)*
- *Islam for Young Girls (Part 1)*
- *Islam for Young Girls (Part 2)*

## Works in English/Arabic:

- *What did the holy Prophet* 🕌 *say?*
- *Qaseedah Burdah*

# NOTES

# NOTES